HADRIAN'S WALL PATH

HADRIAN'S WALL PATH

Anthony Burton

Photographs by Graeme Peacock

Aurum

in association with

NATURAL
ENGLAND

First published in 2003 by Aurum Press Ltd
in association with Natural England
Reprinted with corrections 2007

A catalogue record for this book is available from the British Library.

ISBN-10 1 84513 285 8
ISBN-13 978 1 84513 285 9

Book design by Robert Updegraff
Printed and bound in Italy by Printer Trento Srl

Cover photograph: *The Wall at Walltown Crags*
Title-page photograph: *Broomlee Lough seen from the Wall*

CONTENTS

Circular walks appear on pages 62–65 and 84–85.

HOW TO USE THIS GUIDE

This guide to the 84-mile (135-kilometre) Hadrian's Wall Path is in three parts:
- The introduction, which provides historical background on the area and advice for walkers.
- The Trail itself, split into six chapters, with maps opposite the description for each route section. The distances noted at the head of each chapter represent the total length of Hadrian's Wall Path, including sections through towns and villages. This part of the guide also includes information on places of interest, as well as a couple of short walks that can be taken around parts of the Path. Key sites are numbered both in the text and on the maps to make it easier to follow the route description.
- The last part supplies useful information, such as local transport links, accommodation and organisations involved with Hadrian's Wall Path.

The maps have been prepared by the Ordnance Survey® for this Trail Guide using 1:25 000 Explorer® or Outdoor Leisure® maps as a base. The line of Hadrian's Wall Path is shown highlighted in yellow, with the status of each section of the Trail – footpath or bridleway, for example – shown in green underneath (see key on inside front cover). These rights-of-way markings also indicate the precise alignment of Hadrian's Wall Path, which you should follow on the ground. In some cases the yellow line on these maps may indicate a different route to that shown on older maps; you are recommended to follow the yellow route in this guide, which will be the route that is waymarked with the distinctive acorn symbol ♣ used for all National Trails. Any parts of Hadrian's Wall Path that might be difficult to follow on the ground are clearly highlighted in the route description, and important points to watch out for are marked with letters in each chapter, both in the text and on the maps. *Some maps start on a right-hand page and continue on the left-hand page – black arrows (➡) at the edge of the maps indicate the start point.*

Should there be a need to divert Hadrian's Wall Path from the route shown in this guide, to allow maintenance work to take place or because the route has had to be changed, you are advised to follow any waymarks or signs along the Path.

Distance Checklist

This list will assist you in calculating the distances between your proposed overnight accommodation and in checking your progress along the walk.

location	approx. distance from previous location	
	miles	km
Wallsend	0	0
The Tyne Bridge	4.9	7.9
Heddon-on-the-Wall	10.0	16.1
A68 (for Corbridge)	10.1	16.3
Chollerford	5.1	8.2
Steel Rigg	12.0	19.3
Greenhead	6.6	10.6
Walton	9.7	15.6
Crosby-on-Eden	6.5	10.5
Carlisle	4.6	7.4
Burgh by Sands	6.8	10.9
Bowness-on-Solway	7.9	12.7

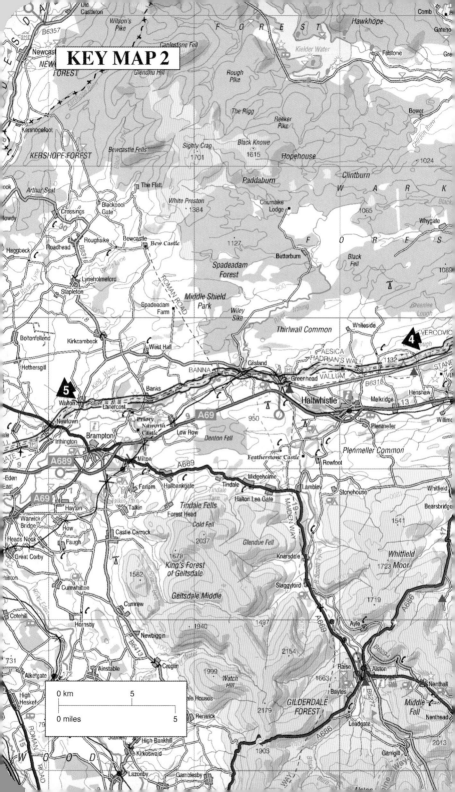

KEY MAP 2

KEY MAP 3

Preface

The twenty-third of May 2003 witnessed a new chapter in the history of Hadrian's Wall with the opening of Hadrian's Wall Path National Trail. The family of National Trails now numbers 15, and, while they all offer the visitor grand vistas and beautiful countryside, Hadrian's Wall Path is in many respects unique. When you walk between Wallsend on Tyne and Bowness-on-Solway, shadowing the historic line of the Wall, consider that this feat has not been possible on a specified route since the end of the Roman occupation of Britain, in the early fifth century.

The Wall is also a World Heritage Site, under the ever-watchful eye of UNESCO, and the very ground that the Trail passes over is itself a Scheduled Ancient Monument. There are also numerous Sites of Special Scientific Interest, an Area of Outstanding Natural Beauty, a National Park, and parts of the Wall are in the ownership of the National Trust.

The advent of the National Trail not only provides wonderful opportunities for walking and exploring our history, but also confers obligations and responsibilities. The Wall remains a fragile resource and the agencies promoting its use for recreation have a duty to protect it for future generations of visitors. Natural England fully supports this aim. Throughout the Trail's planning and development the Countryside Agency, now Natural England, worked closely with many organisations so as to ensure that the management of Hadrian's Wall Path, in looking to the future, also respected the past.

The National Trail's visitors will no doubt stand in awe of the achievements of the Roman surveyors and engineers. Witness the miles of masonry remains and archaeological earthworks! This book will guide you along them, and the tips on when and how to visit the Wall will help you to plan an environmentally sustainable journey along this archaeological treasure. Enjoy it.

Sir Martin Doughty
Chair
Natural England

Hadrian's Wall World Heritage Site

Code of Respect – Every Footstep Counts

National Trail walkers can contribute to the conservation and general well-being of Hadrian's Wall by following the advice and messages contained within Every Footstep Counts, the World Heritage Site's own voluntary code of respect. Hadrian's Wall is the only World Heritage Site in the UK to have such a code and it has been endorsed by all of the government agencies, local authorities, farming, conservation and user groups concerned with the Wall.

1. During the wet winter months the ground becomes waterlogged and this is when the risk of damage to the monument from walkers' feet is greatest. When this is the case, please respect the archaeology. Instead, consider visiting a Roman site or walking one of the many shorter circular walks along the Wall's corridor.

2. If you are only walking a part of the Trail, consider starting your walk at different places or follow a circular route. By doing so, the amount of wear and tear to the Path will be reduced by half.

3. The general rule is never climb up or walk on top of the Wall (a public right of way does exist on top of the Wall at Housesteads Roman Fort, but only for a couple of hundred metres and this is the only exception).

4. Help to take pressure off the Wall itself by visiting a Roman Fort as a part of your visit. They all have visitor facilities and excellent interpretative displays.

5. Only walk along the signed and waymarked paths.

6. If you have a dog with you, keep it on a lead. On National Trust property this is compulsory.

7. Take any litter away with you and never light fires.

8. Close all gates behind you unless it is clear that the farmer needs the gate to be left open.

PART ONE

INTRODUCTION

History of the Wall

Most long-distance paths and trails are designed to make the most of beautiful, wild scenery. This one is different. Not because the scenery is anything but wild and beautiful, but because at the heart of this walk is the most remarkable monument to almost four centuries of Roman rule in Britain. There is a special fascination in following this historic route, a fascination which has exerted its pull on walkers for two hundred years. Modern walkers who complete the route might like to compare their achievement with that of William Hutton, who, in 1801, set off from his home in Birmingham to walk to Carlisle, went the whole length of the Wall, turned round and came all the way back again. He was 78 years old. His account of the journey is lively, but we now know that he got a lot of the history wrong. The aim of this brief introduction is to set the Wall in its historical context. In the popular imagination, Hadrian's Wall, although an immense structure, seems a comparatively simple concept. Stretching from the Tyne in the east to the Solway Firth in the west, it was built by order of the Emperor Hadrian in the second century AD to keep out the barbarians in the north and to protect the superior civilisation of a great empire. This is at best no more than half true. To understand the Wall, one has to look back to the beginning of the story of the Romans in Britain.

Julius Caesar first invaded Britain in 55 BC, then returned the following year, but although he accepted the formal surrender of the British tribes, nothing was done to consolidate Roman authority. It was not until AD 43 that Claudius, an emperor whose position at home was far from secure, decided that he needed a conquest to win popular support and began to look around for an easy option. He found it in Britain, but once he had won his victory, he left the real work of conquering the whole island to others. It was under the governor Agricola that Rome made its greatest advance up through modern Scotland all the way to the Tay, with engineers of the legions keeping supply routes open by building roads up the east coast and the

Milecastle 39, also known as Castle Nick, has the 'playing card' outline that typifies the milecastles along the Wall.

Turret 45A sits at an odd angle to the Wall. Here the walk reaches one of its regular dips, followed immediately by a climb.

west. However enthusiastic Agricola might have been in pursuing his task of conquering the inhospitable country of the Highlands, others, it seemed, did not share his enthusiasm. Rome decided that it was more sensible to try to establish a definite frontier to enclose the most valuable lands. Eventually the army was forced to withdraw from much of Scotland to what would become the new northern frontier of the empire. In mainland Europe, great rivers such as the Danube marked natural divides, but nothing of the kind existed in northern Britain. The most obvious site was the comparatively narrow neck of land between the Forth and the Clyde. However, having achieved substantial victories in Britain in AD 83, troubles in Europe resulted in the recall of one of the four legions in the country. Now the army was spread too thinly to control vast tracts of wild land, so a new border was drawn between the Tyne and the Solway Firth.

Whether or not this was originally intended as a permanent frontier, extra defence works were put in hand. Two important forts had been constructed to guard the roads to the north, at

Carlisle and Corbridge, and they in turn were linked together by a road, the Stanegate. Intermediary forts were then established to protect the east–west link at Vindolanda and Nether Denton, along with a number of smaller forts. There may have been more, but there is no conclusive evidence of this. This was the situation when Hadrian became emperor in AD 117. It was he who decided that it was time to establish a permanent frontier. It was to be marked by a wall that would run to the north of the Stanegate, but extend beyond it to east and west. In the east it would run as far as a new bridge, Pons Aelius, which had been built across the Tyne at Newcastle, while in the west it would extend beyond Carlisle to Bowness.

What we see today is not quite the wall as Hadrian's men built it. For 45 Roman miles (43 modern miles, or 69 kilometres) from the Pons Aelius it was to be built of stone, to a width of 10 feet (3 metres), but the remainder was to be constructed out of turf, in the form of a wall with sloping sides, 20 feet (6 metres) wide at the base. In front of the Wall, to the north, there was to be a ditch, 10 feet (3 metres) deep. The original idea may have been to have the ditch run the whole length of the Wall, but when the builders hit the bedrock at Limestone Corner, they abandoned their attempts to hack their way through, deciding that, at this section at least, the crags of the Whin Sill were a quite adequate defence. We can measure the width of the Wall but not its height, though there is evidence along the way that it probably averaged out at around 15 feet (5 metres). At regular intervals of Roman miles along the way there were what have become known as milecastles, and in between each of these was a pair of smaller turrets, or observation posts. This bare description makes the Wall sound like an insurmountable obstacle, comparable to the city walls of medieval times, with Romans defying the barbarian hordes to the north from behind their ramparts. The Wall was certainly formidable, but this is not how it was seen by the Romans.

Part of the problem comes from the modern names. 'Milecastle' suggests an impenetrable fortress. In reality, they were fortified gateways, so that there were ways through the wall at every single mile throughout its length. The Romans did not defend their territory by holding defensive positions. When trouble threatened, they marched out to meet it, for it was in open combat that the disciplined army performed best. The Wall can be seen as a vast observation platform, from which messages could be relayed to the bulk of the army in the forts to the south. The numerous gates allowed for trade between north and south, but they also allowed easy access to enemy territory if the need arose. As well as these regular openings there were two major crossing points for the military roads to the north. Whatever else it may have been, this was not a permanently closed frontier – not some Berlin Wall of the ancient world. It was part of a system for controlling movement but not preventing it.

The first stage of the construction of the stone wall was setting out the milecastles and laying the foundations for the Wall itself. But quite early on in the process it was decided to reduce the width of the Wall. So one finds a narrow wall, $7^1/_2$ feet (2.5 metres) wide, sitting on foundations for a broader one. So, almost from its conception, Hadrian's Wall was a hybrid: partly constructed of stone, partly of turf, and varying in width from place to place. This was by no means the final change to the plans. Even before the whole line was completed, it was decided that it was not very satisfactory to have all the forts lined up along the Stanegate. If there was serious trouble, the troops would have to be mustered, march perhaps 2 miles (3 km) to the Wall and then make slow progress out through the narrow entrances of the milecastles. So the decision was taken to create a whole new set of forts that would actually bestride the Wall. At much the same time, the Wall itself was extended to modern Wallsend, the lowest possible crossing point on the Tyne. Here, at the start of this long-distance walk, the fort of Segedunum was built and there were to be 11 more forts stretching at roughly 7-mile (11-km) intervals all the way to Bowness-on-Solway. The finished Wall was unique in the Empire. Romans were well used to building defensive structures in turf and timber, but this extensive use of stone, built over such long distances, was a quite remarkable achievement.

Even before the Wall was completed, earthworks were being added immediately to the south of it: a ditch was dug, 20 feet (6 metres) wide and 10 feet (3 metres) deep, with the excavated earth piled up in mounds to either side. This whole structure, the Vallum, has always been something of a puzzle. It is clearly an impressive defence, but it was crossed at regular intervals by causeways. Was there a crossing opposite every milecastle? It seems not, in which case there would have been a detour along the south side of the Wall to get across. Was it a defence against possible attacks from the south, or was it simply part of an elaborate military control system, ensuring that nothing that happened near the Wall went unobserved? There is no clear answer. There is now just one well-preserved Vallum crossing that is readily accessible, and that is in Benwell in Newcastle, but it is not along the line of the walk. It is to be found in a disconcertingly suburban setting at Denhill Park, just south of the A186, across the road from the prominent radio mast. A substantial paved causeway, reveted in stone, crosses the ditch, and there are indications that it was guarded by heavy gates. After the expenditure of a great deal of effort, not to mention a lot of money, a firm, secure frontier had been established that was clearly meant to last. Then, in AD 138, Hadrian died.

The new emperor, Antoninus Pius, set out on a fresh military campaign through northern Britain. Details of this remain vague. Perhaps, like other new emperors, he was anxious to improve his position at home by securing victories abroad; perhaps trouble had broken out among the tribes to the north. Whatever the reason, the legions were on the march again, advancing into Scotland and extending Roman rule. The frontier was shifted again, back once more to that isthmus between the Forth and

The Vallum near Down Hill, one of the places along the walk where this great earthwork can be seen most clearly.

Clyde, and that was the line that was now to be made 'permanent'. Turf earthworks were thrown up, bristling with forts, which we know as the Antonine Wall. Hadrian's Wall was infinitely more impressive, but it no longer had a role. In fact, it was now a nuisance. Gateways were opened up and it seems probable that parts of the Vallum were filled in to make movement easier. History, however, does not stand still, nor is everything that happens neatly recorded for the benefit of historians. New archaeological research is constantly challenging old ideas on the significance of structures.

In the latter part of the second century AD, to simplify a complex series of events, there was an invasion from the north and Roman gains were reversed. There was now an urgent need for some hasty rebuilding of Hadrian's Wall. Forts and milecastles were re-established and the Wall itself repaired. The Vallum was cleared out again and an extra line of earthworks, the 'marginal mound', appears to have been added at this time, using the excavated material, though its significance is far from clear. A new element appeared: the Military Way, running just to the south of the Wall. Campaigning continued and there was to be one more period of extensive development during the reign of Septimius Severus, who became emperor in AD 193 and campaigned in Britain in AD 208–10. The turrets were the first to go, many of them abandoned or completely destroyed. The milecastles were also altered, their entrances narrowed so that they could only be used by pedestrians. Large sections of the Wall were totally rebuilt as a new 'extra narrow' wall, bonded by a hard, white mortar, and it is thanks to the durability of the work done at that time that so much remains for us to marvel at today. Defence and control were now very much centred on the forts. Civilian settlements, or *vici*, developed and thrived around them, and their remains can be seen at sites such as Housesteads.

There were to be other changes over the years, including the rebuilding of barrack blocks in the forts and the gradual opening up of the Vallum. Then, at the beginning of the fifth century, Roman power, which had been declining for some time, began to fall apart and by about AD 410 it was over. Hadrian's Wall was no longer a frontier, but its story was not yet concluded. Civilian settlements eventually grew where military fortresses had once stood. Up and down the Wall the neat, well-cut stones were plundered by local builders, yet the essential identity of

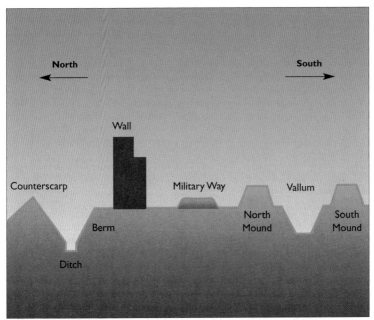

The name 'Hadrian's Wall' applies to more than just the conventional wall itself, made of stone or turf. There are other structures associated with it, and there are now a number of places where one or more of these may be visible but all traces of actual stone wall have vanished. This diagram shows the arrangement, from the ditch – north of The Wall – to the Military Way and the Vallum which lie to the south. All of these features are referred to throughout the description of the walk.

the Wall remained. Then came the Jacobite rebellion of 1745, and the English troops sent north to quell it found themselves hampered by the lack of roads. General Wade was given the task of surveying and building a new network of military roads, and that included a new route from Newcastle to Carlisle, which was actually begun in 1754, by which time Wade himself was dead. With a total disregard for history, much of the new road was built right on top of the line of the Roman Wall, the road we know as the B6318. The antiquarian Stukeley protested, but to no avail. It is fortunate that this act of official vandalism was soon followed by the start of the first real arousal of widespread antiquarian interest in the Wall and the beginning of the conservation movement. Otherwise, there might have been nothing left: no Hadrian's Wall and no Hadrian's Wall long-distance footpath.

There is no need to wonder how Sycamore Gap got its name. It is one of the best-known landmarks along the walk.

Walking the Wall

In general, the aim of this short section is to offer practical advice to help the reader enjoy this Path in comfort and safety. But, in the case of this particular walk, there is one consideration that overrides all others: the need to protect an ancient monument of global importance. Hadrian's Wall has suffered a great deal over the centuries, largely because it has proved an irresistible source of good building stone, ready cut and there for the taking. We are perhaps fortunate that so much has survived, but it is essential that we now preserve what is left. Walking the Wall must involve respect for the Wall. The first rule is simple. However tempting it may be, do not climb on the Wall nor walk on top of it, except for the one short section at Housesteads where it is officially permitted. Every boot that falls on the ancient stones may create only an infinitesimal amount of wear, but repeated over and over again it all adds up to significant damage. We may not see the effects in one year, nor even perhaps in ten, but this is a structure that has been with us for nearly two thousand years. Given care and consideration, it could be with us for another two thousand. We condemn the vandals of the past: it is up to us not to become the vandals of the present. Directions given in this guide will enable you to keep to the authorised route.

The Wall's surviving earthworks are equally important and must also be conserved. The threat of erosion to the path and the ancient monument, which are really one and the same, is an ever-present one. You can help to prevent it if, when you come to a well worn section of the path, you simply walk alongside it, instead of walking in it (like sheep!). This will help enormously to reduce wear and tear to the path and its earthworks. There are other considerations, as well as archaeological ones, that make it important to keep to the official route. On some sections, and especially along the Solway Firth, the Path passes through areas where it is the wildlife, rather than the Roman remains, which needs protection. Needless to say, all the normal rules of behaviour in the countryside, as set out in the Country Code (see inside back cover), apply. This is especially true of farmland, where walkers should cross walls and hedges only at recognised stiles and gates, close gates afterwards and keep to rights of way. As this is mainly livestock country, dogs brought on the walk should always be kept under close control and, where animals are present, on the lead. The area through which this walk passes was devastated by foot and mouth disease in 2001. The farmers need and deserve all the help they can get. The very last thing they need is inconsiderate walkers.

When deciding to walk the Path, the first decision is generally what time of year to go. There are many good reasons for choosing not to go in winter. The central area of the walk is very exposed, and with snow on the ground can become impassable. Even if there is no snow, the region is subject to heavy rainfall, so that conditions underfoot can be very poor, which not only makes walking less than ideal but also adds to problems of wear and erosion. In other words, winter walking is bad news for both the walker and the Path: best to avoid it. For those determined to brave the weather, there is a series of leaflets describing some 40 walks near the Wall, and many of the pay sites are open all year.

When the National Trail project began in 1995, there were many problems to be overcome. The priorities have been to guard against erosion and to create a route that protects the archaeological remains that so many want to see. The British climate being what it is, bad weather can occur at any time of the year, and it is essential to be prepared for it. This is particularly true of this walk, where there are long sections with no shelter available. Good wind- and waterproof clothing is essential. It is rather unfortunate that the word 'anorak' has become associated in popular discourse with nerdish behaviour. Come a wet day on Steel Rigg, with the wind howling and the rain dashing in your face, and it is far, far better to be an 'anorak' than a frozen, wet, shivering wreck. Good footwear is equally important, and although there are no great mountains to climb – the highest point on the whole route is only around the 1000-foot (300-metre) level – the going can be rugged, and in places decidedly squelchy. Walking boots must always be the first choice. There is one hazard, however, which can occur at any time of the year, infrequent but unpredictable. In exceptional circumstances high tides combined with adverse winds can cause flooding of the land along the Solway Firth, including that on the line of the walk. Further information can be found in the description of this section of the walk, and contact addresses and numbers are repeated at the end of the book. If in doubt, check in advance and build extra walking time into your day.

Having decided when to walk the Path, the next obvious question is how long to allow for the journey. Normally, this is

The first part of the walk follows the quayside at the heart of Newcastle, here passing the 19th-century fishmarket.

a fairly easy question to answer, but not in this case: there is so much to see along the way that demands time to explore. To take just one example from right at the start, it is perfectly possible to spend an hour or two at the fort of Segedunum before even setting foot on the Path itself. And, as well as the main line of the Path itself, there are two suggested extra diversions, to Corbridge and Vindolanda, which are well worth making. On any other walk, a week would be more than adequate, but those who really want to explore the history of the Wall should perhaps consider building in extra time. One other important factor in planning the route is availability of accommodation, which is sparse in the central section. Some B&Bs and guesthouses help out by offering a pick-up service, collecting you at the end of the day and dropping you back on the walk the next morning. For hardier walkers, there are youth hostels, bunk barns and camping sites. Information on how to find accommodation is at the end of the book.

27

When it comes to setting out on the walk itself, this guide, with its maps and descriptions, should be all you need to get you safely from one end of the Path to the other. The route is described from east to west, partly because Wallsend, in spite of its name, is a very good starting point. It is easily reached by public transport, and the excellent museum and reconstructed Wall make an ideal introduction. The other reason is a personal prejudice, but one that is probably shared by many others: it is somehow more satisfying to walk out of an urban area into the countryside, than it is to end a great walk by marching into a city.

Direction-finding along the Path is seldom a problem, and there are waymarks at certain strategic points, carrying the acorn symbol that indicates a National Trail. It is a good idea to take a set of Ordnance Survey Landranger Maps with you as an aid to seeing the wider picture and to identify sites some distance from the route, but they are not essential. What is essential is a compass: always useful, but invaluable if really bad weather closes in. Because of the remoteness of much of the Path, walkers will probably need to carry food with them on some days and, much more importantly, plenty of liquid. Everyone has his or her own preference, but this particular walker has always found a water bottle filled from the tap quite adequate, thirst quenching and free.

No one sets out on a walk expecting to have accidents, but they can happen. The first rule is to make sure that someone knows your plan for the day. This is particularly important for those out walking on their own. No one will come looking for you if no one knows you are missing, and on the wilder parts of the walk you cannot rely on casual passers-by turning up to offer help. If you are immobilised, quite the best way of attracting attention is a whistle, so always have one with you. It is not a bad idea to keep it permanently fastened to your rucksack, so that it will always be within reach if needed. Mobile phones have become popular with some walkers, but in wild country one cannot rely on getting a signal.

Accidents are, happily, rare and the vast majority who walk this Path will have a splendid time and get immense enjoyment from the unique mix of history, scenery and wildlife. These warning notes are not meant to discourage, only to ensure that everything does go smoothly in the hopes that the reader will get every bit as much pleasure from this magnificent walk as the author has done.

PART TWO

HADRIAN'S WALL PATH

1 Wallsend to Heddon-on-the-Wall

via Newburn
15 miles (24 km)

Most of this first section of the walk does not keep to the line of Hadrian's Wall, which is mostly hidden under the streets of Newcastle. Instead, it follows the bank of the Tyne through the city and out to Newburn, before turning up to the Wall itself. But even though Roman remains here may be few, this is a route absolutely packed with interest and an ideal introduction to the city that grew up beside the river. There are not only urban pleasures to enjoy, for there is no shortage of wildlife along the way. It was on this stretch of the walk that the author watched a heron continuing on its apparently lazy way, with slow, steady wingbeats, in spite of the angry attentions of a pair of black-backed gulls doing their best to harry it away from their territory. The experience may be different from that of walking through the countryside, but it can be every bit as rewarding.

An obvious starting point is the Wallsend Metro station **A**. To reach the actual walk itself, head down the main road and cross straight over to go down Station Road, once the main approach to Swan Hunter shipyard, where giant cranes dominate the skyline. One of the most famous shipbuilders in the world, it may no longer turn out the luxury liners, but, unlike the majority of its old rivals, it is still at work. Before setting out on the walk, there is an ideal opportunity to gain a first acquaintance with Hadrian's Wall. This is the site of the fort of Segedunum **1**, most of which has been excavated and forms the basis of a new museum. Unfortunately, Buddle Street was built on a line running from the west gate to just north of the east gate, so that only the area between the road and river is on view, but the outline of the remainder is marked by stones. Nevertheless, it is well worth a visit, not least because of the opportunity offered by the observation tower to get what is literally a bird's-eye view of the fort and the layout of the buildings. It is often difficult for the layman to make sense of the pattern of low walls when walking around a site, but here everything is as clear as in a well-drawn diagram. And the tower not only gives a view of the fort, but also opens up a panorama of Newcastle and the Tyne valley. The story of life in the fort is told through a modern exhibition, and there is a

Looking down on the fort of Segedunum from the observation tower, with the cranes of Swan Hunter shipyard in the background.

reconstruction of a bath house. The other main point of interest can be found just outside the fort, close to the west gate. Here the Wall itself has been excavated, and during the work it became clear that at one time it had collapsed and been repaired. To give an idea of how it might have looked when first built, a section has been reconstructed immediately south of the original foundations. It has been built to a height of 12 Roman feet (3.5 metres), which may be an underestimate, and supplied with a walkway and crenellated parapet. There is some evidence that the Wall may once have had a plaster render, so parts have been treated to show different versions of how it may once have looked.

Now it really is time to join the walk. Follow Station Road round the back of the museum, and go up the ramp to join the footpath and cycle track, turning right to pass the former main entrance to Swan Hunter. The first part of the Path uses the track bed of an old railway. It was originally built as an extension of the Blyth and Tyne railway, later absorbed into the grander North Eastern Railway network. Almost immediately the route crosses the spur wall, a short section off the main Wall, which joined the fort to the river bank to close off the line of fortifications. It can be seen to the left of the path, and steps lead down to the excavation – the last chance to see the Wall until the end of this section of the walk.

This urban track has a surprisingly rural feel, as the banks have been sown with wild flowers, now spreading by natural means. In the course of its journey, the old railway crossed a number of streets. Not all the bridges have survived, and where they have been removed, ramps lead down past the surviving stone abutments to the road and then climb back up the other side again. There is never a problem with staying on track. The railway line was built through an area of heavy industry, and it soon reaches a wide, open area where there were once extensive sidings for goods waggons. Here a big yellow crane rears up, looking quite different from the usual shipyard cranes. This is now the Stena offshore terminal, and the crane was built early in the 20th century for lifting immense drums of underwater cables. Beyond this a gas holder appears as a prominent landmark, and the path enters a little area of parkland **B**, where the way divides. Turn left down the ramp to reach the riverside promenade.

The character of the walk now changes. The smell of the sea is in the air, for the river is tidal. At low water, the skeletal remains of wooden barges poke through the glistening mud. Waders, including oystercatchers and redshanks, wander the shoreline, while the river has its black and white contrasts in cormorant and tern. The high grassy slopes above the walk are very scrubby, with patches of rowan and birch, and attract numerous butterflies in summer: one expert recorded 15 different species in a single day. It is all very different from the landscape of tower blocks that can be seen across the water in Gateshead.

Where the path divides, keep to the lower route on the left. Looking back from here, one can see a row of low sandstone cliffs standing above the water. The path leads on into the Walker Riverside Park **2**, where the wild scenery gives way to

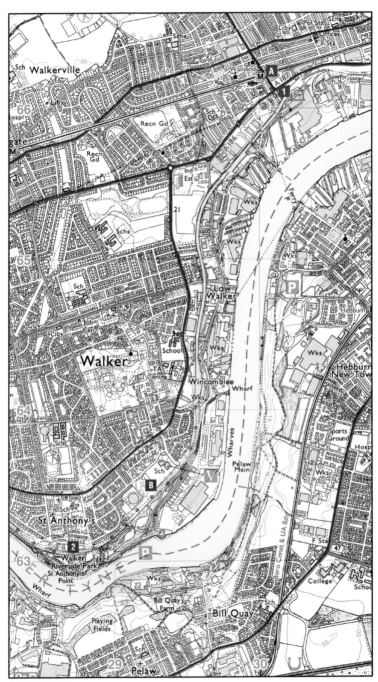

Contours are given in metres
The vertical interval is 5m

33

municipal neatness, with low walls and brick paving, given a vaguely maritime air by unusable bollards. There is road access here, so for a way cars will legitimately be using what still seems to be a footpath. At the end of this section, where the road swings up to the right, still keep on along the riverside walk. Now the buildings of Newcastle come into view, including such easily distinguishable features as St James's Park football stadium. Then the character of the walk changes once again, this time to a cinder track, bounded by shrubs and trees, with masses of broom, alder and sessile oak. Red sandstone pokes through the hillside, while on the far bank there are moorings for the yachts which have replaced the old coal keels on the river.

The walk now enters an area of modern development, The Ropery, with houses built in a bewildering variety of styles, incorporating everything from classical columns to Dutch gables. The name is appropriate, for a map of 1722 shows this whole area covered in rope walks, where the individual strands were plaited to make heavy cables and lines for the shipping industry. Beyond that is the new marina of St Peter's. It is laid out with colonnades along the quay, reminiscent of 19th-century commercial docks, but with apartments and shops instead of warehouses. The boats in the basin vary from modest dinghies to grand yachts and, at the time of the author's visit, there was one traditional, if not exactly local, boat – a spritsail barge that would have spent its working life around the Thames estuary.

The famous Tyne bridges, with the new Millennium Bridge in the foreground.

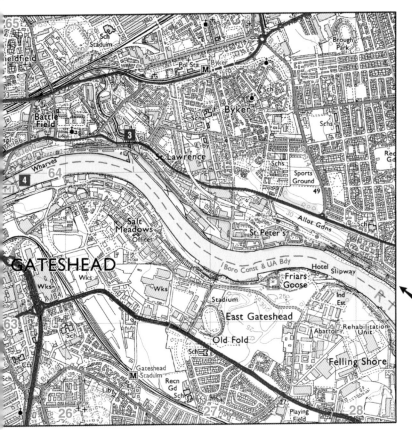

ontours are given in metres
The vertical interval is 5m

After crossing the bascule bridge, return to the riverside and turn first right then left to go down Bottlehouse Street to a T-junction. Turn right past a typical 1930s office building to a mini-roundabout, then turn left down St Lawrence Road, rejoining the riverside walk beyond Spiller's flour mill **3**. When this was built in 1938, it was the tallest flour mill in the world. This is still a working river, with grain coming in for the mill and a sand and gravel wharf on the opposite bank, but it was once much busier – as demonstrated by the old railway lines along the quay. This whole area has gone through immense changes, epitomised by the very impressive Millennium Bridge across the Tyne **4**, linking the Newcastle bank to the old Baltic flour mill in Gateshead. It was instantly christened 'the blinking eye', as the curved walkway can be raised like an opening eyelid to let shipping through.

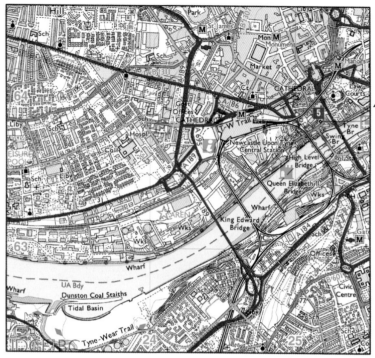

Contours are given in metres
The vertical interval is 5m

The 1949 Baltic building on the far bank, which once held up to 200,000 tonnes of grain, now houses an arts complex.

The walk is now reaching the heart of the city, and anyone coming this way on a Sunday will find the quay crowded with market stalls and shoppers. Up ahead are the famous Tyne bridges, which the walk will pass underneath, and a very varied bunch they are. The first looks like a scaled-down version of the famous Sydney Harbour bridge, which is just what it is, designed by the same firm of Mott, Hay & Anderson in 1925, with a soaring 531-foot (161-metre) steel arch carrying the suspended road deck. Next comes the swing bridge of 1868–76, moved by hydraulic machinery. Going back in time again, we come to Robert Stephenson's famous High Level bridge of 1845–9, after which it is back to the 20th century and the King Edward VII rail bridge of 1902–6, the Queen Elizabeth Metro bridge of 1976–80, and finally the handsome Redheugh road bridge of 1980–3. But there is a good deal to see between the first bridge and the last, and for those with time to spare this is a good place to pause and explore old Newcastle. There are some splendid buildings down by the quay, from the Jacobean timber-framed houses of merchants, such as Bessie Surtees House, to the exotic 19th-century fish market with its exuberant carving showing Neptune gazing down rather smugly on some glum-looking fishwives gutting herring. The most interesting site, however, as far as this walk is concerned, is reached by climbing up one of the steep 'chares' to the 12th-century castle keep, which is splendidly preserved, but more importantly was built on the still partly visible remains of the Roman fort **5**.

The main route continues under the array of bridges as a very attractive paved footpath and cycleway, right alongside the river. Most signs of the city's older industrial life are now to be seen across the river, such as the gasworks and the long, pier-like structure of the Dunston Coal Staithes. One should not perhaps mourn the passing of industry from the Newcastle side, as in this area it consisted of leather factories and lead works, neither of which were particularly healthy in the past. The new industries that have taken their place no longer require specially designed buildings: the emphasis is all on versatility, providing large, adaptable spaces that can be adjusted to meet different needs. The modern offices are basically giant boxes, built on a steel frame, but they have been given a more

The walk passes under the great steel arch of Tyne Bridge.

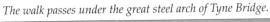

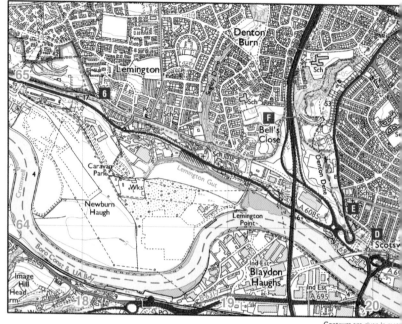

Contours are given in met...
The vertical interval is 5...

traditional outward appearance by the addition of brick cladding, pitched roofs and cosy domestic gables.

The track briefly comes alongside the road at Elswick, then turns away again, following the line of the old working quays with their massive bollards and mooring rings. This is the area that was once dominated by the Armstrong works, which, by the 1860s, were employing some 20,000 men, most of whom lived in the nearby area of Scotswood. It was presumably thirsty work, as there were no fewer than 44 pubs strung out along the Scotswood Road. Now the waterfront houses small apartments, studios and shops, with a scattering of sculptures along the way. But behind them are the cavernous shutes that once connected the upper works to the works on the quay. The riverside walk now comes to an end at a car park **C**.

Carry on to the far side of the car park, then go up the slope and follow the footpath up to the main road. At the time of writing, this section is being affected by a major road-widening scheme, so there will certainly be small route changes over the next few hundred metres. This section will be clearly waymarked, and the general description will still apply; only the details will change. Cross the main road and turn left, continuing past the turning of the B1305. After approximately 90 yards (80 metres), and just before reaching the Vickers works to the south of the road, turn right up the cycle track and footpath through a landscaped area planted with shrubs. This comes out onto another path, created on the line of a former railway: the 1876 Scotswood, Newburn & Wylam. Continue in the same direction but now at a higher level, offering good views out over the open ground to the Tyne valley. The track divides at a point where a footbridge turns left to cross the main road **D**, and where the railway has disappeared into the short Denton tunnel. Bear left along the footpath, turn right at the bollards, then left to reach the main road. Continue up the hill and take the next left turn **E** down a short road to the playing fields. Take the footpath that turns right along the edge of the field, passing the clubhouse, then turn left by the prominent clump of trees to head for the footbridge across the western bypass.

Once across the road **F**, turn left along the track that heads back towards the river, then curves away to the right. A prominent landmark appears up ahead: the Lemington glass cone **6**. Soon the walk returns to the old railway, never far from houses,

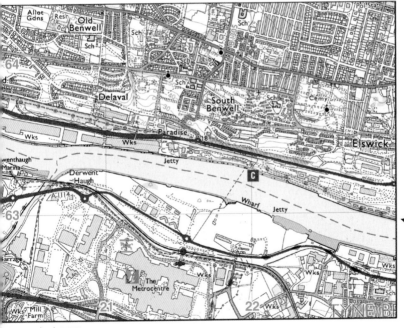

ontours are given in metres
The vertical interval is 5m

but now with a much more rural feel to it. After passing under a substantial road bridge, with a brick-lined arch, the view begins to open out to distant hills, while patches of coarse grassland near at hand are used for grazing horses. It is all very pleasant and also has a place in history, for we have now reached the line of the old Wylam Waggonway, scene of one of the earliest experiments with steam locomotives. Coming into Newburn, the route passes a rather woebegone wooden building, all that remains to mark the site of the once-mighty Spencer steelworks. The path now leads down to the riverside at Newburn bridge.

Continue along the riverside path, passing in front of the Boathouse pub and beyond that where the way divides **G** turn left to keep alongside the river bank on the paved cycle track and footpath. Beyond the playing field turn left to cross the footbridge over the steam to enter the Tyne Riverside Country Park. The walk passes the Visitor Centre, and continues as before along the river bank, past the playground area. Now the city has been very

The riverside walk near Newburn, with the spire of Ryton church poking out above the trees on the opposite bank.

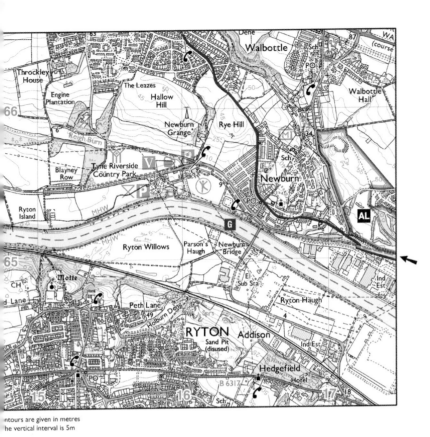

ntours are given in metres
he vertical interval is 5m

much left behind; the opposite bank is covered by trees, and the immediate area round the walk is being improved by the planting of saplings. Almost the only sign of human habitation is a church spire poking out above the trees. The footpath surface deteriorates – or improves if you prefer your paths to have a touch of roughness about them. This is a section made colourful by gorse and broom, shaded by trees and with the river as a constant companion. A little further along, cyclists and riders are banished to a route further away from the bank and walkers have the path to themselves. Birds sing cheerily but seldom put in an appearance, and the occasional swan can be seen drifting lazily along with the current. A dense thicket briefly interrupts the views out to the north, but once past it the scenery begins to change. To the right, there is arable land and a view out to the hilltop village of Heddon-on-the-Wall. Little sandy bluffs rise above the river, and there is a distant prospect of hills up ahead.

41

George Stephenson's birthplace, beside the old Wylam Waggonway.

Gradually the footpath peters out and joins the broad path, the line of the former Wylam Waggonway. This is a historic section of line, for it was here in 1813 that a railway locomotive ran, to be followed by two more: the *Wylam Dilly* and *Puffing Billy*. The locomotives ran past the birthplace of a man who was to be inspired to make a career as a railway engineer, George Stephenson. His cottage is off the route, some 800 yards (730 metres) further down the track **7**.

The track eventually reaches the golf course. Look for a kissing gate on the right **H** and go through it to join the path across the fairway, heading towards the woods. Crossing a little footbridge, an unusual sight appears over to the left – a cricket pitch, complete with handsome pavilion, set inside the golf course. Keep to the broad track up past the pond and continue uphill at the edge of the fine mixed wood of conifers and deciduous trees. There are some particularly grand beech trees, and under the branches ramsons flourish, with their attractive white flowers and pungent smell of garlic. There is a gentle ascent on a track between stone walls festooned with holly and ivy. At the top follow the track as it swings round to the left towards a reassuringly solid stone house with hipped roof, sitting four square among its extensive grounds. The estate wall, however, is rather less reassuring, heavily buttressed but visibly out of true, a sort of leaning wall of Heddon.

Reaching a gate and a row of estate cottages, continue walking uphill past the stone house with the dormer windows. At the top of the hill turn right onto the broad track running along the bottom of the wood. There are extensive remains of quarrying and wide views out over the Tyne valley down to the right. It then comes as a bit of a surprise to arrive at a wealthy suburban area, where some of the builders seem to have had little regard for local styles or materials. Balconies and balustrades flourish, as though the houses were originally designed for the Costa del Somewhere rather than a northern upland village. As the road turns uphill again, the older Heddon puts in an appearance in the form of a solid stone house with mouldings over a Gothic arched door and an integral barn. Another nearby new development has taken up the Roman theme with names such as Trajan Walk and Mithras Gardens. At the top of the hill turn right up Towne Gate, passing The Swan and the little green and follow the road round to the left. Here, after a long absence, is Hadrian's Wall once again 8. This is a good length of broad wall, though not very high, and a section of the Vallum, which appears as a deep depression. The circular structure let into the Wall is not Roman, but a medieval addition, either an oven or a kiln. We shall now be following the line of the Wall very closely for many miles, but it will be some time before it appears this clearly again.

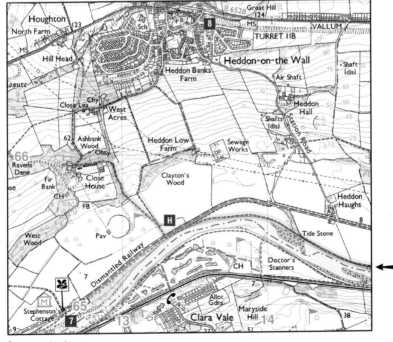

Contours are given in metres
The vertical interval is 5m

43

The Bath House

The bath house played an important part in the life of the forts but was rarely found within the fort walls. There are many examples to be seen along the way, with the best-preserved remains to be found at Chesters. At Segedunum, however, a bath house has been recreated, much as it would have been in Roman times. The house is rather like a mixture between Turkish bath, sauna and social club. Furnaces were used to heat boilers to raise steam and to provide hot air, which not only circulated under the floor as in a hypocaust, the original under-floor central heating system, but also rose up through cavities in the walls to provide the very high temperatures needed in these hot rooms.

The first room, the apodyterium, was both changing room and meeting place, with niches for storing clothes. From here the bathers moved to the frigidarium, which, as its name suggests, was the cold room. Here the hardy could plunge into a cold bath to freshen up at the start of the process, or to cool down at the end after going through the various hot rooms. Because the Romans had not invented soap, they cleaned themselves by rubbing their bodies with oils, using heat and sweat to loosen the dirt and open the pores, then scraped themselves clean with a special instrument, the strigil. The oil was applied in a warm room, the tepidarium, filled with steam. Then it was time to move on to the hottest room, the caldarium, heated directly by hot air from the furnace. At Segedunum there is a small fountain in the middle. A very hot bath was also a part of the process. At the end it was back to the cold room to close up the pores again, rather like modern Swedes jumping into an icy lake after a visit to the sauna. The Segedunum bath house has painted frescoes, looking strangely like suburban bathroom decorations from the 1930s.

Industry and The Tyne

One commodity holds the key to almost everything that happened in the industrial development of Tyneside: coal. It is found in abundance along the North East coast, and lumps of it were broken out of their solid home by waves and weather to litter the shore as 'sea coal'. There was enough coal close to the surface along the banks of the Tyne for a brisk trade with London to develop. A document of 1228 refers to 'Sacoles Street' near the Thames, which still exists in a modernised spelling as Seacoal

Lane. In 1292, when the monks of Tynemouth Priory were being taxed to pay for Edward I's crusade, they were recorded as having collieries at Tynemouth itself and at Wylam, bringing in an income of just over 80 shillings a year. In the 18th century work began on mining at Wallsend in what was to develop into a major colliery with, at its peak, eight shafts being in use in the area. Some of the remains can be seen very close to the start of the walk.

Much of the coal went south, carried down the Tyne by barges or keels, then loaded into colliers, as the sea-going vessels were known. It was a logical development to begin building the vessels locally, and a shipbuilding industry soon began to develop. Inevitably, with time, the easily won coal was worked out and ever-deeper mines opened up further inland. This created a brand-new problem: how to get the coal from the pithead to the river. The answer, discovered early in the 18th century, was the waggonway or railroad. At first this was simply a track laid out with wooden rails, offering a far better surface than the crude roads of the period. As the journey from the mines was generally downhill, little effort was required from the horses pulling the loaded waggons, and the main occupation of the man in charge was operating the handbrake on the last waggon to keep everything under control. In time, iron rails replaced wood, and one of these old tracks, the Wylam Waggonway, is followed to Newburn as part of the walk. It was on this line that William Hedley began experimenting with a steam locomotive, the *Wylam Dilly*, which trundled past the cottage where a young man lived who also worked in the local mines. He took a considerable interest in the proceedings: his name was George Stephenson. It was he more than anyone else who brought the steam railway out of the limited world of collieries and set it on its way to becoming the principal transport route of the 19th century. It was his son, Robert, however, who designed one of the most striking monuments to the railway age: the high level bridge that crosses the river at Newcastle, with its two decks, one for road traffic and one for rail. But there are also reminders of the continuing importance of the coal trade to be seen along the way. A short way upstream from Stephenson's bridge, on the south bank of the river, are the Dunston coal staithes, an elevated structure along which the coal waggons were rolled to discharge into keels waiting on the river.

In many industrial processes, fuel was the most important element in terms of bulk and weight, so that it was usually cheaper to bring the raw materials to the coalfield for processing, rather than take the coal somewhere else. One of these industries was glass making, which uses coal, sand and alkali. There was no problem with coal supplies, and sand was brought back by the colliers as ballast. Alkali was made from wood ash. Glass-making in the area was begun on a large scale in the 17th century. Sir Robert Mansel wrote in 1615 that he had 'contrary to all men's opinion' and 'after the expence of many thousand pounds' established a glassworks in Newcastle. In the 18th century, glass was made in huge, conical furnaces. The molten glass was taken from a central furnace by men working inside the cone and blown. It was then either shaped to make glassware or flattened out for window glass. One of the few surviving cones, probably built in the 1780s, is a prominent feature on the approach to Newburn. This was not the only industry in this area. Ironworks were also established, and the ironworks begun by John Spencer at the beginning of the 19th century developed into steelworks employing some 1500 men. The walk passes the site, but little of the building survives.

In 1727, Daniel Defoe had noted of Newcastle: 'they build ships here in perfection, as to strength and firmness and to bear the sea'. A century later, the Tyne was the third-largest shipbuilding area in Britain, but the greatest days still lay ahead. It was in making ships of iron and steel that the shipyards of the Tyne came into their own, building a third of all the world's great vessels. Newcastle was at the forefront of technology, and no better example can be given than the story of Charles Parsons and the steam turbine. Having developed his turbine on land, Parsons set about trials of a marine engine. He designed an experimental vessel, appropriately called *Turbinia*, which in 1897 shattered all previous speed records and astonished naval dignitaries by dashing across the assembled British fleet at the Spithead Review at a speed of 34 knots. This sleek little vessel has a permanent home in the Newcastle Discovery Museum. That was just the start. The turbine was soon developed and set to power the mighty *Mauretania*, launched in 1907. It was very much a local effort. Steelwork was supplied from Spencer's and the ship was built by Swan, Hunter & Wigham Richardson. Swan Hunter still make ships at Wallsend, right by the start of Hadrian's Wall.

The other great name in engineering in the North East was William George Armstrong. His first claim to fame was the development of hydraulic machinery, and by 1837 he was building cranes by the riverside at Elswick. One of his hydraulic engines was installed to move the swing bridge that crosses the river in

The Armstrong coat of arms can be seen along the way at Elswick.

the heart of Newcastle. From cranes he moved on to armaments and the rifled cannon. He started making ships' guns and ended up building the warships as well. Armstrong eventually became Vickers-Armstrong, who still have a factory in the area. The riverside walk passes right through what was once the heart of the great industrial empire at Elswick. All these developments were based on the river, and river improvement soon became essential. Once there was a great loop between Scotswood and Newburn, but that was straightened out to create a new channel – all part of the development of industrial life and an industrial complex that served the whole world. One cannot help thinking that the Romans would have approved.

2 Heddon-on-the-Wall to Chollerford

15¹/₄ miles (24.5 km)

After visiting the exposed section of the Wall, retrace your steps towards the green and turn right just before the Women's Institute onto the track in front of the row of stone cottages. The track goes downhill, and, although it is far from obvious, you are actually walking on a filled-in section of the Vallum. Passing the churchyard and the memorial garden, the lane leads back up to the road again **A**. Cross over and take the road running behind the Three Tuns, signposted to Harlow Hill. If it was not very clear that one had just been walking along the line of the Vallum, it is even less obvious that one is now walking on top of the Wall itself. The only indication that there is anything of archaeological interest here at all is the slight dip on the far side of the stone wall, marking the presence of the Wall

The first substantial section of the Wall to be seen since leaving Wallsend is here at Heddon-on-the-Wall.

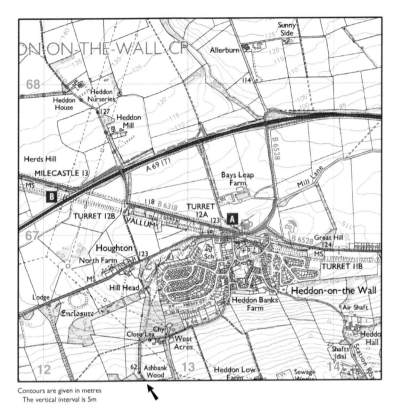

Contours are given in metres
The vertical interval is 5m

ditch. Although this stretch of the walk is on a road, it is far from unpleasant: a stroll through arable farmland that seems to support an abundance of bird life, and on my visit included the appealing appearance of a pair of greenfinch. This quiet road swings right to cross the busy A69, and then turns sharply left alongside the main road. It is a short acquaintance, for the minor, but busy, road soon turns away again **B**. Look for a stile on the left, cross it and then turn right to continue following the line of the road at the edge of the field. A short way along is a raised, grassy platform, all that remains of Milecastle 13, but at least the shape is clear. Squared-off stones in the field bank may well be remnants of the Wall itself.

This section of the walk goes down a pleasant avenue of trees. This is traditionally common land, though it is not obvious why. The likeliest answer is that this was a green lane that developed over the centuries along the line of the Wall. Rather vague indentations in the land to the left indicate the presence

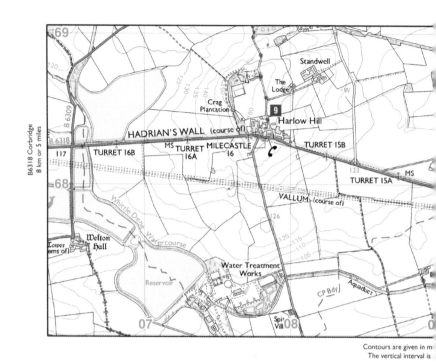

Contours are given in m
The vertical interval is

of the Vallum. The line continues through a series of gates, heading towards the prominent clump of trees, and after a slight climb a view opens out across the Tyne valley. On reaching the trees, turn left and head for the gate just in front of the farm buildings. Cross straight over what can be a surprisingly busy minor road and take the gate opposite to return to a field path. There are indications of earthworks in the field, but they are not easily interpreted when walking along. In fact, these are the remains of the fort of Vindobala, or Rudchester. In the 18th century it was described as a well-preserved fort, but the builders of the military road took away the stones and farming destroyed much of what was left. Cross over the field to the far corner by the road to continue following the line of the road once again. Although the traces of the Wall may seem disappointingly scarce and difficult to interpret, the walk itself is very pleasant, with grassy fields, many bright with flowers, and there are tremendous views over the countryside to the south. Cross the steel bridge over the stream and continue on the field path beside the road as far as the next boundary **C**. The path makes its way past the house and gardens at the small cross-

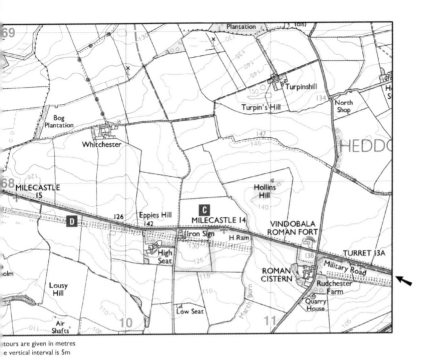

tours are given in metres
e vertical interval is 5m

roads before returning to the edge of the field near the crest of the hill. Here the course of the Vallum is very close at hand, although how clear this is will depend on the time of year and whether crops have been planted. The easiest way to spot it is to look to the west, where a sort of wavy line can be seen on the horizon. Carry on along the field edge until you arrive at the steps up to the road **D**. Cross over and join another field path, but this time to the north of the road.

The walk continues in the same direction, but now following the very clearly defined Wall ditch. There is gorse and hawthorn, and a wide swathe has been left between ploughland and the hedge, allowing wild flowers to flourish: coming this way in spring, the cowslips were prolific. The road hopping at least serves as a reminder that the Wall itself really is under the road, as you can see the Vallum to the south of it and the ditch to the north. The path now remains alongside the road all the way to the garage on the edge of Harlow Hill. Leave the field and follow the pavement through the village. There is one curious feature, the little church, which looks sadly dilapidated **9**. Take a peep around the back and you can see why. A large door has been knocked into

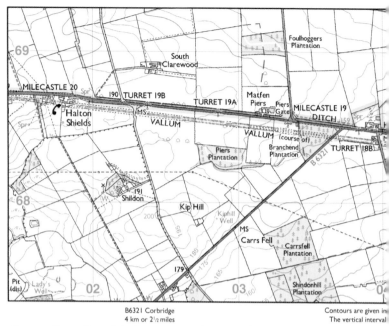

B6321 Corbridge
4 km or 2½ miles

Contours are given in
The vertical interval

the north wall and it is now serving as a barn. Roughly a hundred yards past this ecclesiastical barn, leave the road and rejoin the field path heading towards the reservoirs. Now, instead of the path offering views either to south or north, vistas are opening up all around. There is a sense of spaciousness, though the landscape is still dominated by the patterns of fields and farms.

The reservoirs offer a chance to pause and watch the bird life out on the water. Botanists will be rather more interested in the patch of grass between the path and the reservoir. This small area is untouched by pesticides or fertilisers, and as a result flowers proliferate. It is a reminder of how meadows once were, but now sadly seldom are. The odd little castellated building across the road is the original reservoir pump house. The next section of walk, after crossing the B6309, takes us back to the ditch and a surfaced path of stone flags. There is a good reason for this. The ditch takes surface water from both the fields and the road, and it would be a sorry morass if simply left alone. Go through the gate to the right of the ditch and continue along beside the ditch. The section ends with steps up to the road. Follow the road past the Robin Hood, then return to the field path. At the end of the cottages turn right to cross the footbridge over the ditch and continue the field walk, with a brief interruption to cross the minor

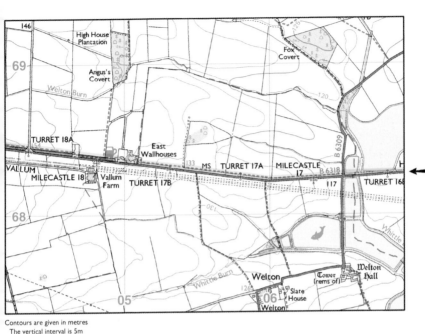

Contours are given in metres
The vertical interval is 5m

road. Just before Wall Houses the Path turns to the right over a stile and runs northwards for about 250 yards (225 metres) before turning sharp left to run behind the buildings and back to rejoin the footpath beside the road where the B6231 joins from the left. The footpath beside the trees and stone walls leads on to the driveway of Matfen Hall, marked by a pair of rather grand gateposts, and now it is time to cross the main road once again.

Go through the gate and down the steps, still following the line of the road, and now the view that was being enjoyed of the land to the north is obliterated and a new view opens up to the south. Once again, there are the merest traces of the Vallum in the fields, which would probably go unnoticed if one was not expecting to find something on this side of the Wall. The route continues to the next interruption, a minor road. Cross the steps in the wall and continue along the verge path for a short way: less pleasant than walking through fields, perhaps, but there is compensation in the much-improved view of the surrounding landscape. There is an obvious crossing point, after which the footpath continues on the north of the road, passing a farm sheltering behind an immense stand of beech trees. This is a long, steady climb, but at the end there are some of the best views to be found so far along this stretch of the walk.

At the layby **E** cross the road yet again, and now there is a very clear view of the Vallum earthworks in the field to the south. Where the verge path ends, cross the stile and continue on the footpath inside the wall. Now having joined the field, the Vallum looks even more impressive. It goes on getting even better as the walk goes around the clump of trees, bringing you closer to the earthworks **10**, and, perhaps for the first time, one gets an impression of just how formidable a barrier the Vallum was. Altogether this makes for a magnificent and exciting scene, where, even if the Wall itself is still hidden, one has a real feeling for great works having been achieved. There are promises of more excitement up ahead with a view of Halton Castle in the distance. The route skirts an area of shallow quarries and heads back up to the road. Continue to the corner of the field next to the road to return to the now-familiar pattern of walking just inside the field next to the wall.

Somewhat incredibly, the Vallum, which had appeared in such spectacular fashion, has suddenly vanished again. The reason can be seen in the corrugated field effect, the fossilised remains of medieval and later ploughing. The pattern of ridge and furrow is typical of the period, and when the land was put

Halton Castle, a mixture of gaunt medievalism and urbane domestication, as seen from the circular walk to Corbridge.

Whittington

168

169

Milk
Hill

Air
Shaft

Down
Halton 192 Hill MS
Red House

E 209

Carr Hill

Port Gate

TURRET 21A
(site of)

VALLUM

Carr Crags

MILECASTLE 22
(rems of)

TURRET 21B
(site of)

VALLUM
course of

186

F

MILECASTLE 21

10

Downhill Quarries
(disused)

Carr
Houses

ONNVM
ROMAN
FORT

Stagshaw Kennels (Spr)

Spr

162
158

158

168

191/186

99

Halton Castle
(remains of)

Low Houses

Halton

00

140

01

Contours are given in metres
The vertical interval is 10m

to grass the old field pattern was preserved. An even more disturbed pattern of earthworks appears up ahead, centred on the ground around the driveway leading down to Halton Castle. The regular oblong pattern represents the outline of the fort of Onnum, but there are complications introduced by patterns of old ploughland and what look very much like the house platforms of a medieval settlement. The most striking feature here is the grand gateway marking the start of the formal approach to the castle. This is the starting point for the circular walk through Corbridge **F** (see pages 62–65).

The main walk continues towards the ladder stile and then rounds the little copse. A simple stone clapper bridge crosses the stream, after which it is a return to a walk beside the wall. This continues until a set of steps is reached, leading up to the road. The walk continues on the grass verge as far as the roundabout. Cross over the A68; looking at its straight line disappearing into the distance it comes as no surprise to discover that it is aligned along Dere Street, the Roman road from Corbridge. A ladder stile to the left of the Errington Arms leads back into the fields and the walk heads off to follow the prominent earthworks of the Vallum. The nature of the walk is beginning to change, the rough grass

55

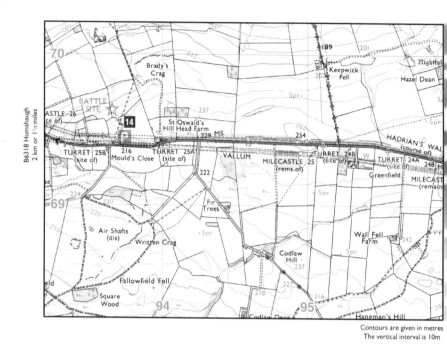

Contours are given in metres
The vertical interval is 10m

giving the landscape a feeling more of moorland than arable farmland – a feeling soon confirmed on the author's walk when a pair
of partridge suddenly shot up from among the tussocks with a
whirr of wings. The next stile takes you to the far side of the fence,
away from the Vallum, though it remains a very imposing feature
in the landscape. This is a pleasant walk through the fields, which
leads to a conifer plantation. Go through the gate and turn right,
then left on the path running beside the wall next to the road.
Woodlands such as this are notoriously soggy places, and the
worst of the wet patches, where walking was even more difficult
due to tussocky grass, have been overcome by laying flagstone
walkways. Like most such plantations, the trees are close set and
effectively shut off the view, so that it is something of a relief to
emerge at the far side to be faced by some very attractive countryside. The walk continues in a straight line, crossing the road to
reach an area dotted with gorse, with the Vallum once again
appearing to the left. There are remains of small quarries in the
fields, and the well-defined outline of Milecastle 24 **G** sticks out
from the side of the road. Just beyond that, a stone stile leads up to
the road. Cross straight over and carry on, joining the field on the
far side, now following the line of the Wall ditch.

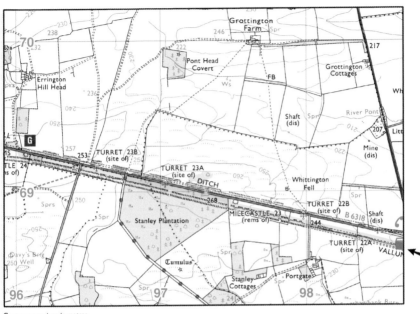

Contours are given in metres
The vertical interval is 10m

The change of side brings a change of scene: now there are panoramic views to the north, and those who come this way regularly claim that on a good day there are views of the Cheviots. It would, one suspects, have to be a very good day. But even if the Cheviots fail to appear, this is still splendid countryside. Nearer at hand, there are some obvious earthworks, the result of quarrying. The Roman ditch, however, is unmistakable and very deep. Running alongside the north (field) side of the ditch is a ridge of spoil left by the Roman builders. This is itself an important archaeological feature so please resist walking on it and help to prevent erosion by keeping to the level ground to the north. History apart, this is a good area for walking, with soft turf underfoot and a lively population of birds. Even if they are not always visible, you will be accompanied by the sweet song of the skylark, the call of the lapwing and the mournful cry of the curlew.

Just before reaching the farm, look out for a gate on the left and steps up to the road. Follow the path in front of the farm and tearooms and then rejoin the path across the fields. The next section crosses the site of the 7th-century Battle of Heavenfield. One side was led by King Oswald of Northumbria; the other was an alliance between Cadwallon of Gwynedd and Penda of Mercia.

In his history Bede portrayed it as a victory for Christianity over paganism, but it was more complex than that. Cadwallon was, in fact, himself a Christian. It would perhaps be more reasonable to represent it as part of the long struggle between Celts and Anglo-Saxons. Nevertheless, this became an important site for Christianity, and the victorious King Oswald was to become St Oswald. The church commemorating the battle **14** stands in its own little enclosure and is well worth a visit, though it is a comparative newcomer, only built in 1737.

From the wooden cross, turn diagonally away from the road to the wall and continue in the same direction parallel to the road, but now on the opposite side of the Wall ditch. In fact, the path is very close to the line of the Wall, though it remains invisible. The path continues across the face of a tree-studded hill. The road has made a slight detour, but it is rejoined at the top of the hill and the walk continues beside the boundary wall. On reaching the broad trackway **H**, cross over the road; there in the field to the south is the Wall itself **15**, and a particularly interesting section it proves to be. Here one can see the foundations of both the broad Wall, with a section of the curtain wall rising above it, and the narrow Wall. Look out, too, for a culvert near the point where the width reduces. Several of these were built to stop water collecting and undermining the foundations. This is much more rugged country than has been met so far, and a line of crags can be seen just to the south.

In the next field, the earthworks show that at last the whole Wall really has emerged from under the roadway, and one can begin to take in the relationships of all the various parts. Looking back from the end of the field, for example, provides an outstanding view of the Vallum, with an oak neatly set between the banks. After that the walk goes through an attractive area of woodland, mainly birch, with undergrowth of ransom and lords and ladies. At the road turn left, passing a small manmade waterfall feeding a drinking trough. Where the woodland comes to an end, the view opens out over fields, dotted with some magnificent trees, so that the whole effect seems typical of eighteenth-century parkland. Continue down the lane to the junction with the main road, near the village of Wall **I**. Cross over the road and turn right to follow the path on the verge. After approximately 500 metres, look out for a stile on the right with an English Heritage sign **J**. This leads to a path to Brunton Turret **16**. It is well worth making this short diversion of no more than a few hundred metres.

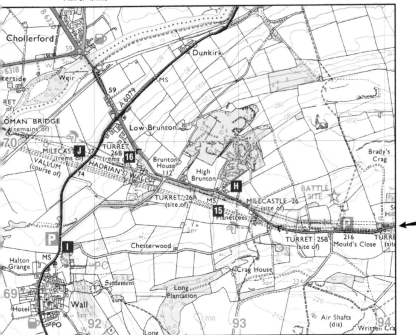

ntours are given in metres
he vertical interval is 10m

This is a good spot to pause and take a closer look at the physical remains, in order to try and get an impression of how the scene would have looked in Roman times. The Wall rises to a considerable height at this point, with as many as six courses of stone still standing in places. The turret itself rises even higher, to a maximum of 11 courses, and is one of the best-preserved on the entire Wall. Turrets such as this were simple structures and were supplied with just a single entrance to the south, with no gateway through the Wall to the land to the north. The massive stone doorstep in the south wall is still in place, and there are grooves which held the vertical slabs that formed the doorjambs. Not enough of the turret has survived to give any indication of how high it rose, how many floors it contained, nor how it was roofed. A wing wall to the east encloses a small, badly worn altar.

Retrace your steps along the side of the wall to the road. Cross over and turn right, then left down the main road to Chollerford Bridge. This is a remarkably handsome five-arched stone bridge with very prominent cut-waters. It was built in 1775 following the great flood of 1771, which demolished its predecessor.

The Forts

The numerous forts strung out along the Wall present very different faces to the walker. At Segedunum it is possible to climb a tower and see the whole pattern of excavated buildings laid out as if in a diagram, while at the far end the fort of Maia has been lost from view beneath the buildings of modern Bowness-on-Solway. In between there is a fascinating mixture of sites that have been thoroughly excavated and others where there is little to see apart from bumps in a field. Each makes its own contribution to the understanding of how these structures would have appeared in Roman times.

The forts vary in size from less than 1 hectare to almost 4 hectares, and the first obvious difference is that some are built straddling the Wall, while others lie entirely to the south of it. The former, such as Chesters, had three twin-portalled gates to the north of the Wall, and two single- and one double-portalled gates to the south of it. The rest, such as Housesteads, had four double-portalled gates, one to each side. In plan the forts are oblong with rounded corners and contain the remains of a variety of buildings. The most important, at the centre, was the headquarters, usually facing east with a walled forecourt and an imposing building, generally decorated with appropriate military carvings such as representations of Victory and Mars. An important feature was the underground chamber, which acted as a strong room.

The other very impressive building was the commander's house, which would normally have had a number of luxury features, including a hypocaust to keep it comfortable in winter and a private bath house. The commander was a man of considerable rank; he would have had his family living with him and they would expect a lifestyle not very different from that which they enjoyed at home. The men were originally housed in barracks, where a 'century' of 80 men would be housed, with their centurion enjoying the privacy of his own room. Cavalry regiments would have stabling for their horses. All forts had their own granaries, which often appear far grander than the barracks.

Other buildings might have included a bath house for the men, sometimes inside but more usually outside the perimeter, and a hospital. There were also shrines, altars and temples near, or inside, the fort. Water was an essential, and aqueducts often brought the supplies from a considerable distance. There are remains of stone tanks at some sites, and Housesteads is notable for its well-preserved latrines, which were hygienic and regularly flushed out.

Inevitably, a civilian population came to gather around the fort, providing essential services – and services of a more dubious nature. In time, a regular settlement would grow up, known as the *vicus*. Often evidence of the presence of the *vicus* is difficult to see on the ground, and it is often hard to be certain whether what can be seen dates from the period of Roman occupation or later. Cultivation terraces are evident, for example, on the slopes by the fort at Housesteads.

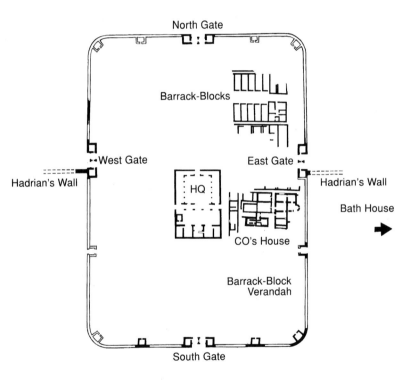

Chesters Fort, built to house a cavalry regiment, with three of the main gateways giving access to the land north of the Wall.

CIRCULAR WALK TO CORBRIDGE

7¹/₄ miles (11.7 km)

Although the main object of the walk is to visit the important Roman fort and military headquarters at Corbridge, there is a lot more of interest to see along the way. From the gateway by the main road, take the main drive down the avenue of sycamore towards the castle, noting the indications of ridge and furrow along the way. Stay with the drive as it swings around the left-hand side of the castle, shielded at first from view by a tall hedge. Just beyond the house is a small church, which served the village of Halton **11**. It is a very simple building, partly dating back to Saxon times, and the main architectural feature is the round-headed chancel arch. But it is the roof beams that make this building very unusual. Normally, even in the simplest building, they will have been squared up even if left undecorated, but here they are tree trunks left virtually in their natural state. Stones from a Roman temple are said to have been used in the south wall at the chancel end, but today only the faintest traces of carvings are visible.

Carry on down the roadway, going steadily downhill past the pond. Looking back, there is now a clear view of the house. It is easy to see how the 'new' house has been tacked onto the old castle, which itself has been domesticated by the addition of large windows. Fine, tall chimneys add a finishing touch to a very attractive set of buildings. The quiet lane runs down between hedgerows brightened with red campion. At the road junction **A** turn right; this is still a pleasant stroll through farmland. Swinging round past a patch of woodland, there is a view over to the left of another grand house, Aydon Castle. At the next road junction **B** turn left into another peaceful lane, this time lined with some rather grand trees, including a horse chestnut which has spread its branches right across the road and into the field beyond. At the foot of the hill, a footbridge crosses a stream by a ford, an attractive spot apart from the noise of traffic on the busy A69. The lane goes under the A-road and continues on towards Corbridge. Then a rather surprising sight appears beside the road: a pair of pottery bottle kilns **12**. These can be visited via a little gate just past the house. They are beautiful, shapely structures, gently curving to the narrow outlet at the top. Walk inside and look up, and try to work out just

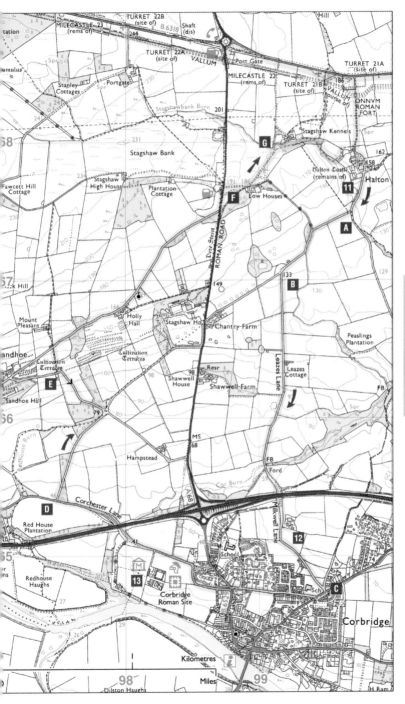

Walk continues overleaf

One of the extensive granaries at Corbridge, showing the under-floor channels which allowed air to circulate.

Continued from previous page

how the bricklayers managed to achieve this sinuous shape. Originally, there would have been a central furnace, around which the ware would have been packed for firing. This was the Walker Pottery; it had nothing to do with graceful vases for the mantle-piece, but mostly made such mundane items as sanitary ware and bread bowls. There are also the remains of a pair of rectangular kilns, rather more typical of potteries in the North East.

The road now continues down into the outskirts of Corbridge to meet the main road **C**. Turn right and then right again down St Helens Way, past the school. After a little way the view opens out over to Corbridge itself and the square church tower. Carry straight on across the main road, following the sign to Corbridge Roman Site. The road passes a very grand red-brick house, goes through a Z-bend, and arrives at the entrance to the Roman site **13**.

The visit begins at the museum, which does an excellent job in explaining the history of the site and its excavations, as well as displaying many of the finds. There are a number of carvings, often quite crudely executed, such as a rather muscle-bound Hercules slaying the hydra. The pottery, however, is very interesting, not least for the realistic decoration. One piece shows a blacksmith at work, and, apart from the clothes, he could be any blacksmith at work today. Outside is the site itself, which has had a complex history. The original fort was probably built by Agricola between AD 70 and 80, but was sited about half a mile (1 kilometre) to the west and was short-lived. It was replaced by a turf fort on the present site which was refurbished, and from around AD 130 construction of the stone fort began. It was to become a military headquarters and later a supply depot, with the Stanegate running through the middle. As such, it had to have extensive granaries, with raised floors allowing air to circulate underneath to keep the grain dry. A rare survivor is a little mullioned aperture, part of the ventilation system. Later, this became a civilian town and there is evidence of the sophistication of Roman life, including a cistern supplied by an aqueduct. But by the time the water reached the cistern, it would have been stale and insipid, so it was passed through an aeration channel to put the sparkle back in. Everywhere there is a complex pattern of foundations, representing houses and workshops, and part of the site now undulates like a frozen sea as a result of subsidence into the fort ditches. For those who are taking this walk and want to do the fort justice, be warned – it is not a place to hurry around.

After the visit, return to the road, turn left and cross the A69 again. At the woods **D** turn right towards Sandhoe, then left up the hill from the crossroads. As you near the top you can see a series of ledges in the fields to the right. These are cultivation terraces, known as strip lynchets and extensively used by medieval farmers on hilly sites such as this. At the top of the hill turn left, and after a short way turn right across a stile **E** into the field and continue uphill beside the wall. At the road turn right; you get a view out over the Tyne valley and more strip lynchets appear in the fields. The road ends at a junction with the main road, the old Dere Street. Cross over and turn left, then right opposite the house **F** onto the bridleway. Where the way divides by the houses, turn left onto the tarmac track through rather scrubby woodland. Where this bends, turn right by the footpath sign **G** onto a path through the wood. This is a pleasant walk through the trees to a broken-down section of boundary wall. Here the path goes down to the pond. Follow the little stream as far as the footbridge, cross over and continue in the same direction but steadily climbing the bank to reach a gate and another footpath sign. Go through and continue up the line of the fence; the castle comes into view again over to the right. Cross over the stiles to rejoin the drive and return to the main gate by the road.

Geology and the Wall

The underlying geological strata of any region have a profound effect on the scenery, but along Hadrian's Wall an extra element comes into play. The geology also had a direct effect on how and where the Wall was built, and even on how it has changed through the years.

The eastern side of the region is dominated by the Great Northern Coalfield, where layers of shale, sandstone and coal have been deposited, one above the other. These were laid down in the Carboniferous period, some 300 million years ago, but the landscape was given a far later shaping in the Ice Age, or the Pleistocene, which only ended in northern Britain a few thousand years ago – an eye-blink in geological time. The glaciers scoured the land and left behind a layer of debris, a combination of clay, sand and gravel. The landscape that emerged is generally flat, with just a gentle rise of low, rounded hills. It proved an ideal terrain for wall builders. There were no real obstacles in the way, so that following a straight line presented few problems. Very conveniently, there were ridges with thick bands of sandstone close to the surface, easily quarried and ideal for building.

The coalfield peters out somewhere near Heddon-on-the-Wall, and a new type of rock appears alongside the sandstone. Limestone was formed over millions of years when the land was covered by sea and the skeletons of marine creatures settled on the seabed, where they were compacted together. There was still a plentiful supply of good, easily worked sandstone, but the limestone was also useful. It was burned in kilns and was adopted by the Romans to make a very durable lime mortar, extensively used in rebuilding the Wall during the reign of Septimius Severus. In later years, lime was widely employed in agriculture, and more modern lime kilns are very much a feature of the landscape hereabouts.

The central section of the Wall runs through a very much more complex region. To the west of the North Tyne, there is still the same pattern of alternating bands of sandstone, limestone and shales, but here there was a different pattern to the ice flows. The ice attacked the harder rocks, creating a series of ridges with hard-edged scarps, while the softer rocks were simply ground away, leaving hollows. Into this sandwich a newcomer literally erupted. Magma from deep below the crust forced its way upwards through fissures and cracks, crystallising as it cooled to form dolerite. The result was the Great Whin Sill, a ridge of very hard rock running east to west and falling away in a steep, north-facing escarpment. This was a fine natural defence, and the most dramatic section of Hadrian's Wall marches along high above the cliffs. The Romans, however, found the hard dolerite a difficult rock to handle. Quarried stone proved intractable, and at Limestone Corner the attempt to create a ditch through the bedrock was rapidly abandoned. When it came to digging the Vallum ditch, the engineers chose a line at the foot of the hill, which also offered easier ground for digging.

The next geological change occurs near Banks, where soft red sandstone was heavily eroded by glaciers and then covered by a deep layer of sediment. As a result, the rough uplands begin to give way to a more gentle landscape, laced with rivers and streams. It was in this area, where good building stone is not so readily available, that the Stone Wall originally gave way to the Turf Wall. When the Turf Wall was in time replaced by stone, the red sandstone had to be brought from quarries several miles away. This was to have unfortunate consequences for archaeology. If the Romans sometimes found they had to travel some distance to find a source of suitable building stone, their successors had no such problem. It was all there ready for them to use, and, even better, already dressed in neatly squared blocks. So the local people simply carried the stone off in cart-loads for their own houses and barns.

The final section of the Wall runs across the salt marshes that border the Solway Firth. It is not an altogether flat landscape. The retreating glaciers left behind low hillocks of boulder clay, and it was on these that the settlements developed. But in general it is a land of wide vistas and broad expanses of water. Once again, stone was scarce, and it seems that some of the stone for the Wall may even have been brought from the northern shore of the Firth. And, inevitably, over the centuries the Wall stones were removed and reused. A notable example can be seen at Burgh-by-Sands, where St Michael's Church stands on the foundations of one of the fort buildings. The builders were not too concerned about which stones were used, so that the image of a Celtic head can still be seen carved into a stone in the east wall of the chancel. If the long processes of geological change had left this area with decent building stone, we might never have seen a pagan god staring out from the wall of a Christian church.

The central section of the Wall passes through an area well endowed with good bui

stone, as here at Walltown quarry.

3 Chollerford to Steel Rigg

via Chesters and Housesteads
12 miles (19.3 km)

Once across Chollerford Bridge, turn left at the roundabout, down the B6318, keeping to the right-hand side of the road. The walk passes a farmhouse with an elegant, long, round-headed window, an unusual embellishment for a farm. Then the entrance to Chesters Fort appears on the left **17**, which is not a site to be missed. This site has a particular importance in the story of the rediscovery and preservation of the Wall. The area was part of the grounds of a country house, home to John Clayton, who began the excavations here, literally outside his own back door. The museum displays his finds at various sites along the Wall and is a memorial to his efforts. The physical remains on site are of considerable interest. There are two barrack blocks, which consist of a series of rooms, each intended for eight men, and a larger room for the centurion – an arrangement that has been copied

The attractive approach across the fields to the bridge over the North Tyne at Chollerford.

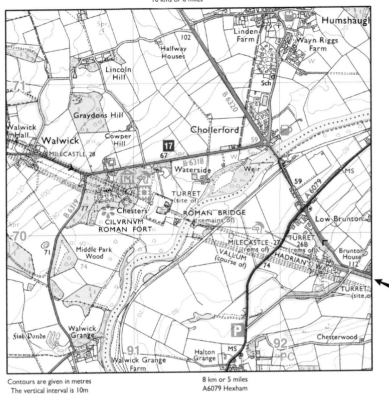

Contours are given in metres
The vertical interval is 10m

8 km or 5 miles
A6079 Hexham

by armies more or less ever since. The headquarters building includes an underground strongroom, which when excavated had a stout oak door – this disintegrated on exposure. The commanding officer's house is comparatively luxurious, with hypocaust and a personal bath house. The main bath house, however, is the most imposing building on site, with walls rising above head height. The layout will be familiar to those who have begun the walk at Wallsend and visited the reconstructed bath house at Segedunum (see pages 30–31). Before leaving the site, walk down to the river bank to see the remains of the Roman bridge and the partially exposed guard house. The river has shifted its course through the centuries and the remains of more considerable abutments can be seen on the opposite bank. There is good evidence that a water mill was incorporated into the tower. The first bridge, built under Hadrian's rule, had eight piers, but it was rebuilt in the third century by Severus as a much more monumental affair with three arches.

Black Carts, where the walk enters the Northumberland National Park and has climbed up to meet a section of the Wall.

Returning to the walk, continue straight on past the road junction. More grand buildings appear, home to horses not people. This is a stud farm, and the buildings are topped by a neat little clocktower and enlivened by shaped gables. Keep on the road to Walwick village, with single-storey cottages, of the type normally found in nearby Scotland, and rather more substantial farms. Take the next right turn by Walwick Cottage **A** up the quiet lane, past the barns, and look out for a ladder stile in the wall on the left. Continue across the field with the fence on the left, passing the high walls that surround the grounds of Walwick Hall. Once clear of the wall, take a slight diagonal to the left towards the corner of the field, marked by a prominent tree. In the next field continue along beside the fence and hedge. At the end of the field, turn left to go around the quarry, passing the earthworks of the Wall ditch. The next section of the walk lies within the Northumberland National Park. Cross over the road and enter the little copse. Turn right and keep following the line of the field wall around the edge of the woodland. Ahead there is a long line of the Wall visible. After passing through the gate please head for the line of the roadside wall and follow it.

Once across the approach road to Black Carts **18** there is the first long section of the Wall itself to appear for some time. Here, too, are the remains of a turret, built for the broad Wall. Continue along the line of the Wall, crossing the minor road. The Wall ditch now appears as a deep 'V'. The stonework of the Wall disappears to be replaced by a bump in the ground, but this is excellent walking up to a trig point at the top of the rise which provides excellent views over miles of open country. By the site

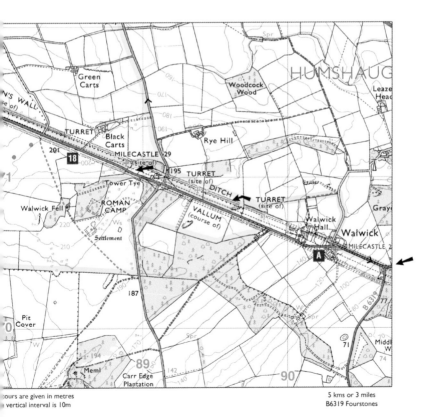

cours are given in metres
vertical interval is 10m

5 kms or 3 miles
B6319 Fourstones

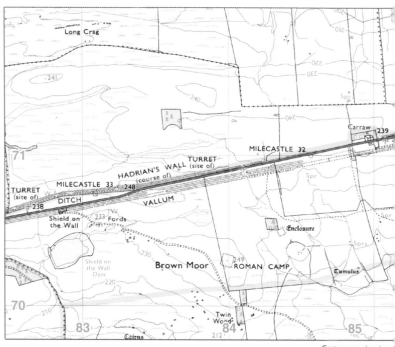

Contours are given in me
The vertical interval is

of Milecastle 30 the Wall turns to the south, following the natural contours of the land. It runs down to the road, and the Vallum can be seen on the opposite side. This is an interesting spot known as Limestone Corner **19**. The ditch, which has been such a prominent feature, stutters to a halt at an area of tumbled stone blocks. The Romans, when faced with resilient rock, simply gave up trying to cut a way through, though, as we can see, they were not sufficiently deterred to abandon the Vallum. At the fence cross the stile and continue the walk on the northern side of the ditch. Opposite the sign to Brocolitia cross the road to reach the stile opposite and continue the walk along the field to the car park. This is beside the site of the fort of Brocolitia, which was clearly planned and built after the Wall, as it lay on top of the infilled Vallum. Turn left onto the obvious path and follow it round to the right beside the fence to reach the Mithraeum **20**. This temple to the Persian god Mithras would have been a gloomy place, lit by lamps to create a very theatrically mysterious interior, in which the statues to Mithras himself and his associates Cautes and Cautopates would have been highlighted.

74

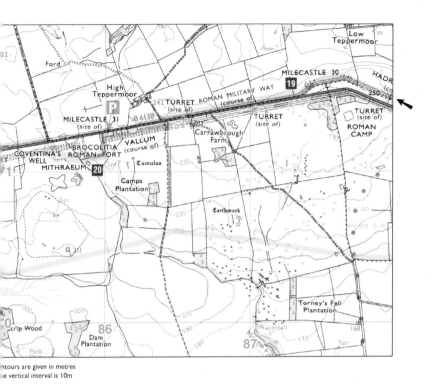

tours are given in metres
e vertical interval is 10m

These are now represented by modern reproductions, though the originals can be seen in a modern recreation of the temple in the Newcastle Museum of Antiquities. There was also a well, sacred to the goddess Coventina. Leave the Mithraeum by the stone-flagged path, crossing the burn on a simple clapper bridge, and then turn right to return to the road.

Cross over the road to join the path at the edge of the field, which continues along the line of the Wall ditch for some way, apart from a brief diversion around the farm buildings. This is all rough grassland, and the bird calls are those associated with upland regions – skylark, curlew and lapwing. They have to compete, however, with the noise of road traffic, but there is a temporary reprieve as the road swings away to the south and the walk follows the line of the ditch, past the remains of Milecastle 33. It may not appear at first glance to be the most spectacular of the surviving milecastles, but it is an excellent example of the philosophy that underlies the planning of the route. Before the path was completed, the remains were not on any public right of way, and there was a great deal of Roman masonry still in situ.

75

Some of the finest scenery along the whole walk is to be found near Housesteads, where the Wall swoops up and down the undulating hills.

Following a complete stone-by-stone survey, an expert mason carried out the necessary repointing. A timber broadwalk was then laid across the western threshold and new turves placed on top of the masonry. The aim has been to maintain the green setting of this milecastle with a minimum of disturbance. It is now up to walkers to do their bit by not clambering over the turf-capped remains. There is a brief reunion with the road, before the latter turns decisively away to the south, leaving the way ahead through open and increasingly wild countryside. Here one can see substantial remains of a turret. The route is now heading towards the prominent group of trees behind the farmhouse on the skyline. The square enclosure with trees marks the site of a milecastle. The walk is now going steadily uphill, with an ever-steeper drop falling away to the north.

Approaching the cottage, leave the line of the Wall, aiming for the trees to the right of the next cottage. Cross over the farm track and pass through the gate to enter the woods. This is an attractive stretch, with the woods perched on the rocky slopes of Sewingshields Crags. Once out at the far side, you are very much back with the Wall itself and Milecastle 35 **21**. The outline of this is clear, and the individual rooms are well delineated. One notable absence is any sign of a gate entrance to the north. There was a gate originally, but it was blocked in, presumably because it would have been of very little use at this airy site on top of the crags. In any case, the general nature of the Wall has changed quite considerably now. The crags provide their own defences to the north, and the Vallum can be seen swinging well away to the south, where the work of digging ditches would have been considerably easier away from this stony ground.

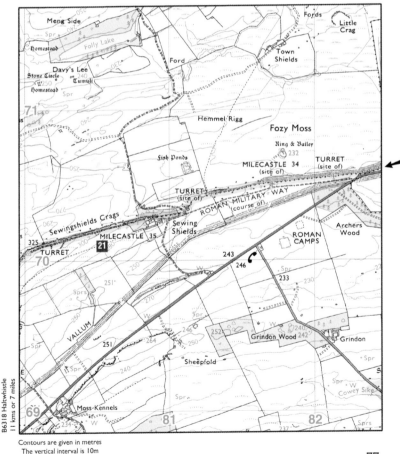

Contours are given in metres
The vertical interval is 10m

This is an altogether splendid section of the Wall and a stretch of superb walking as well – an unbeatable combination. The climb ends at a trig point, and now the view opens out to the beautiful open countryside and Broomlee Lough. Here is one of the most spectacular views of the Wall, snaking away into the distance, following the high ground to take advantage of the natural defences of this dramatic landscape. The view also provides all-too-clear evidence that the next few miles are going to have something of a switchback character, dropping steeply down into hollows and climbing just as steeply back up the other side. There is a brief interlude as the walk passes through a little wood, and then it is down to the Knag Burn and the site of one of the main gates through the Wall **22**. There are guard chambers on either side, and the stream goes through the Wall in a conduit. The track now crosses the Wall, continuing through the gateway up the opposite side to Housesteads. To the south there are signs of the civilian settlements that grew up under the protection of the fort. They are not always easy to interpret. The more obvious features are the cultivation terraces and fields, while other lumps represent the *vicus*, the civilian settlement of houses, workshops and shops laid out in streets. Housesteads itself is one of the most popular places along the Wall and can be visited by leaving the line of the walk to reach an entrance to the south **23**.

It is easy to see why Housesteads is so popular. It has a magnificent site and, with its well-defined ramparts, still looks like a fort; plus, of course, it is right on the Wall itself. To the Romans this was Vercovicium – the place of good fighters – and one can easily imagine that only the toughest troops would be sent to this bleak, isolated spot. By now, the arrangement of the forts will be familiar, but there is one feature here that has not been met before, and always sends children into fits of giggles: the communal latrines. These were very sophisticated, with water fed from a cistern into a channel at foot level to wash the excrement away through a duct in the walls. The *vicus* buildings to the south were described by Hutton, when he visited the site two centuries ago, as having 20 streets, located just by the south gate. The north gate was originally approached by a ramp, but given the nature of the landscape, it was probably little used. The eastern entrance gate has gatepost sockets and the typical double arches, though the south was blocked in at some time before the fort was abandoned. The western gate is comparatively well preserved, with a considerable amount of

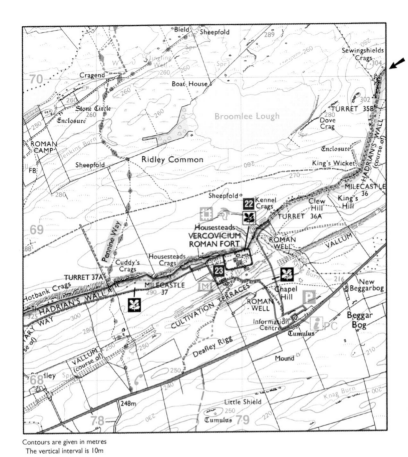

Contours are given in metres
The vertical interval is 10m

the central pier still standing, and the remains of a stone water tank by the guard house. One of the buildings has been tentatively identified as a hospital.

The section of the walk beyond Housesteads is the only place where walking on top of the Wall itself is officially accepted. Having said that, it is actually rather more pleasant to use the footpath alongside for this stroll through the woods. This is a famously scenic section of the walk above the Housestead Crags, passing Milecastle 37. This milecastle is particularly interesting, traditionally built by the Second Legion to Broad Wall specifications. The first striking feature is the north gate, which still has the piers in place, as well as the beginning of the arch. From this it is possible to work out the height of the gateway and to make an assumption from that of the likely height of the Wall,

The remains of the arched gateway in the north wall of Milecastle 37.

which must have been somewhere above 15 feet (5 metres) high. Comparing this with Milecastle 35, the puzzle is why there was a north gate at all since 37 stands above an equally steep drop. At the south gate there are post holes and sockets for the double doors, with a doorstop in the centre. The remains of the rooms for the guards can also be seen.

The next stage of the walk involves more steep rises and falls, but life for the walker has been made easier by a set of rough stone steps. A climb to the brow of the hill reveals a stunning view over Crag Lough, and it is easy to see where the name comes from, as the rock faces drop sheer to the water. The path leads down towards the lake. Cross straight over the farm track where the way divides **B** and cross the stile on the right to take the path up into the woods. Steps aid the walker on the last part of the climb, but the effort is well worth making as once the trees begin to clear there are even better views down over the lake. It is the sort of place that one is tempted to linger to enjoy the tranquillity, watching a swan drift slowly across the water, or looking up to find a bird of prey hovering over the rough landscape, perhaps with an eye for one of the young rabbits that are regular visitors to the walk and its surroundings. Now the walk descends to Sycamore Gap, where the path goes through a gap in the Wall before clambering up the other side. It seems a long way down to the Gap – and an even longer way up. Immediately to the south is the old Roman Military Way, offering an easier route than the one offered by the walk, which continues its pattern of climbs and descents. But once again the extra effort is rewarded with excellent views and the archaeological remains. Milecastle 39 is known as 'Castle Nick', from the fact that it has been built into a natural nick in the hillside, and differs from 37 in that the longer sides are orientated north–south instead of east–west. The walk passes to the south of the milecastle. Now it climbs up above Peel Crags but the stay at the high level is a short one, to be followed by the steepest descent yet. Cross the Wall at the top of the hill. A rough stone pitched path has been constructed, winding down the face of the hill to Peel Gap and one of the very few turrets visible on this stretch of the walk. This reflects how many were demolished in Roman times. The path leads back up to the top again, passing a ladder stile on the left. Do not cross it, but keep following the line of the Wall. It is worth pausing to look back at this very scenic section of the Wall. This section ends by the Steel Rigg car park, and there is a walk to Vindolanda from here.

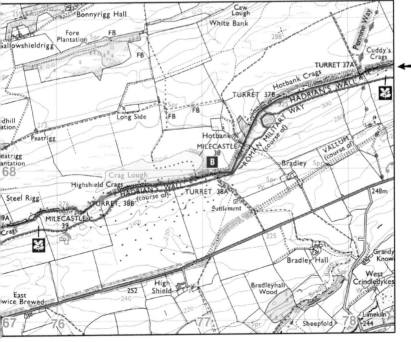

ntours are given in metres
he vertical interval is 10m

Milecastles and Turrets

In between the forts, defence was reinforced by milecastles, built at intervals of one Roman mile, with smaller turrets in between. On modern maps, the milecastles are numbered from 1 to 80, starting in the east, with the intervening turrets numbered in a similar way but as A or B after the nearest eastern milecastle, so that, for example, Turrets 37A and 37B lie between Milecastles 37 and 38. By no means all or even most of these structures can still be seen and recognised, but a surprisingly large number are still to be found and these provide regular punctuation along the way.

The milecastles can perhaps best be thought of as defended gateways. There would be an entrance, in the form of a double gateway topped by an arch, in both the north and south walls, with the occasional exception such as Milecastle 35, which is all but inaccessible from the north. Putting together the evidence from a number of sites, we know that there were stairs to a higher level, probably to a tower above the north gate. The milecastles were like miniature forts, with thick defensive walls and often employing massive stone blocks in the gateways them-

A typical milecastle arrangement, showing the two gates, the central passageway, accommodation for the men and stairs to the top of the Wall.

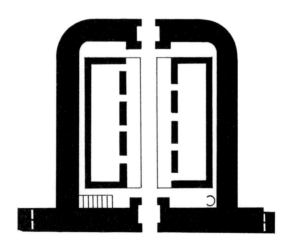

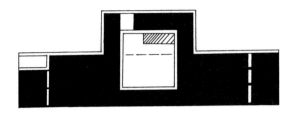

The diagram shows a turret with two integral spur walls, suggesting that it was built first and then connected to the Wall itself later.

selves. Because nothing has survived above the first few courses, there is inevitably a good deal of speculation about how they looked when in use, but illustrations of the time show similar stuctures in other parts of the Empire, in which the walls are crenellated. As with the forts, the milecastles are rectangular in plan, with rounded corners: some have their long axes parallel to the Wall; some at right angles to it. The orientation may have depended on which legion was responsible for the construction. In many of the milecastles there is evidence of internal buildings for the men, suggesting that anything from 8 to 32 could have been stationed in a milecastle at any one time. Their main job would have been to control movement through the Wall, and to collect taxes where appropriate.

The turrets are altogether simpler. Here the only entrance is to the south, and one presumes these were little more than look-out towers. There are a lot of questions that necessarily remain unanswered. What proportion of the milecastles and turrets were roofed over, and were the roofs flat or pitched? There is some evidence of window glass having been used, but nothing to suggest how many windows there were, nor where they were situated. Nevertheless, they remain among the most atmospheric of all the surviving structures, if only because they often turn up in some of the wildest countryside and occupy some of the most dramatic sites. Life in the forts clearly had its comforts: there was precious little of that commodity in some of these lonely places.

Circular Walk to Vindolanda

3³/₄ miles (6.1 km)

The distance quoted above is for the walk to Vindolanda and back again. It is possible to undertake a genuinely circular walk by using the Military Way, but there is very little to be gained, other than having to do one of the most strenuous sections of the whole walk twice. This is by far the simplest method of reaching Vindolanda, and it has the added advantage of coming down to Once Brewed, where there is a pub, accommodation and a visitor centre, which provides information about the National Park and the Wall. So many walkers will be turning off the Path here anyway.

The walk begins at the top of Peel Gap. Coming from the top of the hill, instead of following the main line of the walk round to the right, head straight on to the ladder stile, then head towards the cottage and a second ladder stile, leading to the road **A**. Turn left and follow the road downhill. Cross straight over the main road and continue on the minor road, still going downhill. Where the road divides **B**, turn left; the very straight road is aligned along the Stanegate. After a short distance the stump of a stone pillar can be seen in the field on the left **24**. It may not look very impressive, but this is a Roman milestone, and a second example can be seen near the Vindolanda car park. Stay with the road down to Vindolanda **25**.

The fort predates the building of the Wall. It was built *circa* AD 85 and was connected to Carlisle and Corbridge by the Stanegate. It was built of wood and regularly renewed as the timbers rotted, until it was eventually replaced altogether on a quite different alignment by the stone fort. The story of Vindolanda is still being explored, as archaeologists continue their work. Already a huge amount of invaluable material of all kinds has emerged, much of it the stuff of everyday life – shoes and textiles, jewellery, pots and glassware, and surprising items such as a lady's wig. But by far the most important are the written documents from the early wooden fort. These were written in ink on wooden tablets and over thousand have been recovered, mostly dealing with the running of the fort, but including reports on the activities of the local population, the *Brittunculi* – the wretched Britons. Those who build empires never seem to have a high opinion of the peoples they conquer.

The site is complex. The playing-card pattern of the stone fort is clearly defined, with its four gates and recently excavated south wall standing to a height of 6 feet (2 metres). Inside are the usual ranges of buildings, though there are also remains of a number of circular huts. These are reminiscent of the round huts of Iron Age Britain, and it has been suggested that they were used to house native families held as hostages during the British revolt of the early 3rd century. The *vicus* is outside the fort, but mainly within the confines of the older timber fort.

Down by the south-west corner of the early fort, sections of Turf and Stone Wall have been reconstructed. Originally, much of the Wall in the west was built of turf, with timber palisades and milecastles. A section has been recreated as it might have been, with a timber tower rising above a gateway. Next to it is a length of Stone Wall and a turret. They are necessarily speculative: the Stone Wall and tower, for example, are shown as crenellated, but no one knows whether the actual Wall was treated in this way, nor even whether there was a walkway along the top, though it is logical to assume that there was. Near to these replica buildings a small cemetery has been discovered, with two mausolea.

Outside the south gate to the stone fort are the remains of the military bath house and an open-air museum. After the visit, retrace your steps to return to the main walk.

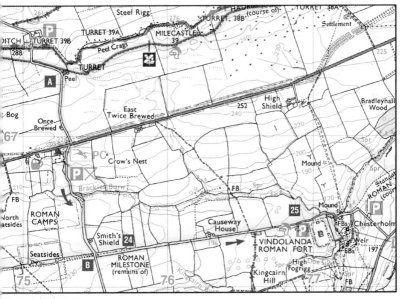

ontours are given in metres
The vertical interval is 10m

An aerial view of Vindolanda and the long straight line of the Stanegate. Patterns of

...idge and furrow can be seen in the surrounding fields.

Religion

This is a subject which seems remarkably complex to anyone living in the 21st century, but it tells us a lot about the kind of people who built and garrisoned Hadrian's Wall. If they had all come from Rome itself, one would have expected to find them adhering to their native Roman beliefs, much as the British Army in India remained strictly Christian, though surrounded by a Hindu and Muslim population. But the Roman Empire was not like the British Empire. The soldiers were recruited from different parts where they had their own beliefs, and in later years the legions included many native Britons, who were initially devoted to their own British and Celtic gods. This was never seen as a problem by the Roman rulers, who were not only tolerant of others' religious beliefs so long as they represented no threat to Roman civil rule, but were quite capable of assimilating new gods into the Roman pantheon. So one finds shrines to Celtic gods built in the classical style, complete with Latin inscriptions; these can be seen all along the Wall. The water goddess Coventina, for example, has her own small temple at Carrawburgh. It had a central well, which, when excavated, was found to contain over ten thousand Roman coins, as well as dedications from both officers and men. One of the best-preserved shrines can be seen near the Vallum crossing at Benwell, dedicated to Antenociticus. Here a statue of the god was set in an apse with altars to either side, and these can be seen in Newcastle Museum of Antiquities, with replicas on view at the site.

Inevitably, however, the Roman gods themselves were given pride of place and official recognition, with Jupiter, as the leading deity, being held in great esteem. Prefects dedicated altars on their own behalf and on behalf of their cohorts at the forts, generally with the simple inscription IOM: Iuppiter Optimus Maximusque – Jupiter the best and greatest. There were other altars to other gods, Mars being an obvious military favourite. There were gods who were particularly honoured in certain places, as Hercules was at Housesteads, and others who were adopted by special units such as the cavalry. Then there were the gods who came to Britain with the units recruited in different parts of Europe, but which soon appeared in Roman guise. The German god Thincsus was honoured at Housesteads as Mars Thincsus, and he appears in a sculpture as a very Roman figure.

The most exotic element was the introduction of mystical religions from the east, notably Zoroastrianism, which first appeared in the Persian Empire. The prophet Zoroaster or Zarathustra preached a dualist religion, in which there is a perpetual war between a good god and an evil god. It was based on an even older Indo-European religion in which the forces of light were led by Mithras, who killed the great bull that epitomised evil. Mithraism was a very esoteric cult, and it put great emphasis on the role of individual men personally helping in the battle against evil. It was an exclusive religion with complex initiation rites, and something of its secretiveness can be sensed at the Mithraeum at Carrawburgh. It is small and dimly lit. There is an anteroom, or narthex, where the uninitiated could wait, and beyond that the temple itself with side benches, originally flanked by sculptures representing the opposing forces of darkness and light. The exclusivity of Mithraism ensured that it was a cult for officers, not for men.

There was one last religion that was eventually to triumph over all its predecessors: Christianity. It was adopted by Constantine in the early part of the 4th century and subsequently became the official religion of Rome and the army. It seems likely, however, that the old paganism survived in spite of the bans. The new god was simply assimilated into the old order, much as others had been. There is very little evidence of Christian worship along the Wall in Roman times, but a good deal of evidence to show how later Christians used the Wall. Lanercost Priory, built by the Augustinians in 1166, used Wall sandstone in great quantities, managing to incorporate both an altar to Jupiter and to the local god Gitanus into the fabric. It seems anachronistic to us, but this would have seemed perfectly natural to the Romans.

4 Steel Rigg to Walton

via Gilsland and Birdoswald
16¹/₄ miles (26.3 km)

From the car park, cross straight over the road, and the Wall is temporarily invisible, though the Wall ditch remains a prominent feature. This remains a pleasant walk across the fields on gently rising ground to a trig point at 345 metres, the highest point on the Wall, and although the general line of the walk thereafter is downhill, there are still a good few dips and climbs to come. Altogether this is a fine, wild section of country, a rocky landscape where the Wall soon appears once again in very substantial form. In spite of the ups and downs, the walking itself is very good, over short, springy turf. Milecastle 41 stands at the top of one of the steep slopes, a superb position commanding views over a wide expanse of countryside. Now there is a steep little descent to the road, followed by the inevitable, if gentler, climb back up the other side.

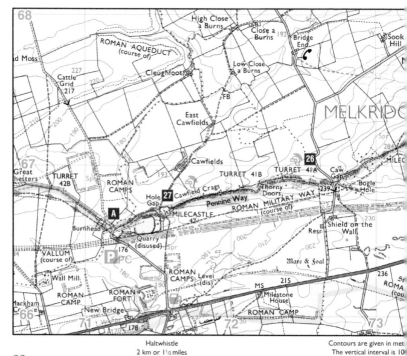

Haltwhistle
2 km or 1¹/₂ miles

Contours are given in met
The vertical interval is 10

Once again the climb brings back the views and the Wall. Turret 41A **26** was one of many demolished in Roman times, the three walls away from the Wall reduced and the space between filled with stone blocks. This happened to many turrets, but is rarely as obvious as it is here. A long length of the Wall itself can clearly be seen, snaking across the hills, while over to the left there are good views of the Vallum down in the valley. The section of Wall beside Cawfield Crags is particularly impressive and provides a vista of the open land to the north with its scattering of farms. Milecastle 42 **27** is very clear, with walls standing to a good height. The main features are the two gateways, built with very substantial blocks in the north. These may well have been needed to support a tower above the gate. The walk continues past a former quarry, which has eaten away at the remains of the Wall, though the Vallum remains intact to the south of the lake that now occupies the old workings.

Walk around the north side of the lake and leave the quarry area by taking the driveway up to the road. At the road **A** turn right over the bridge and then left at the stile to rejoin a field path

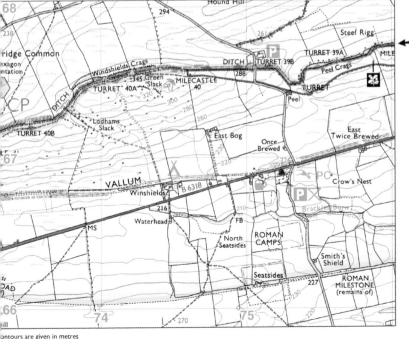

Contours are given in metres
The vertical interval is 10m

past the cottage. The Wall has vanished again, and now the walk is back on pastureland beside the Wall ditch. Over to the left are signs of old ridge and furrow, and to either side of the walk there are other faint earthworks, which represent the remains of Roman camps. Take the stile to the left of the farm, leading into a field and the site of Aesica or Great Chesters fort **28**. This is a comparatively small fort and little remains to be seen apart from the outline of the outside walls. The most interesting feature can be found by turning left off the walk towards the eastern side of the south gate. Here is a squat pillar, with a very indistinct carving of a jug or ewer. This is an altar, the real thing rather than a replica, and the only one of its kind still surviving in situ on the Wall.

Leave the fort at the north-west corner and continue with the ditch to your right, heading gently uphill towards the stone

Looking back from the heights of Steel Rigg to the Wall clambering over the rocky cliffs above Crag Lough.

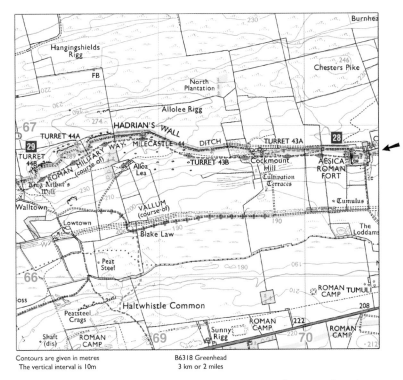

Contours are given in metres
The vertical interval is 10m

B6318 Greenhead
3 km or 2 miles

house by the trees. Enter the wood and turn right onto the obvious path which swings left to follow a line between the mixed woodland and the more densely packed conifers. There are unconsolidated remains of Wall in the wood, and an enterprising farmer has purloined a Roman milestone to use as a gatepost at the western end. At the other side, the nature of the landscape changes once again to rough, stony moorland, and although the Wall is scarcely detectable, the Wall ditch is quite clear and still forms a very obvious boundary in the landscape. The nature of the walk in this section changes all the time. Looking back, the Wall can be seen, striding along above the crags, and sections keep appearing and disappearing along the way. The path continues alongside the spine of a hill, avoiding the ridge itself which conceals the buried remains of the Wall. Each little climb seems to reveal a new prospect and the way ahead can be seen running along a line of crags, once again with a number of dips to cross. At Turret 44B **29** the Wall turns through a right angle to cope with the changing terrain, so the builders were able to save on stone and effort by letting the Wall itself form two sides of the turret.

Little knolls where the underlying rock pokes through the turf make for a splendidly varied landscape at Walltown Crags.

Head slightly south towards the flagged path and stile. Cross over the farm track and then head back uphill for a walk along the top of Walltown Crags. Turret 45A **30** provides a splendid viewpoint, and down in the valley to the south the Vallum is now a very distinct feature. The next section must have proved very difficult for the builders as the Wall had to be fitted in wherever it would go between rocky knolls and the escarpment edge. The result is very impressive, and here the Wall stands in places at well above head height. This section of Wall comes to an abrupt end as the field wall turns south, heading down towards the valley and another lake in another former quarry. Follow the wall downhill, but do not continue along the line of the wall as it climbs up above the quarry. Instead, enter Walltown Quarry via the ladderstile and take the gravel path round the north side of the lake. This area is being transformed into a National Park recreation area, with little waymarked trails, and the reedy pools are already home to a variety of waterfowl. Carry on down to the road and turn right. After approximately 100 yards (90 metres) turn left, just before the cattle grid **B**.

A short diversion can be made here to the fort of Carvoran and the Roman Army Museum 31. Instead of turning right at the road, turn left; the entrance is little more than 100 yards (90 metres) away. The museum is run by the Vindolanda Trust, and once again features reconstructions, this time including the inside of a barracks. There are artefacts of various kinds illustrating all aspects of military life.

The main line of the walk continues over the fields, on the north side of the ditch. At the next field boundary continue downhill towards the ruined keep of Thirlwall Castle 32. At the bottom of the field turn left along the farm track, and follow it round in a U-bend to reach the footbridge. The 14th-century castle stands on a steep-sided motte and enjoys a commanding view across the valley. Most of the stones used in its construction were taken from the Wall. Once over the bridge, turn left to take the field path beside the stream. This pleasant interlude ends when the stream is crossed again and the path goes straight over the railway to the road. Turn right along the road, passing the entrance to the golf course, and then look for steps on the left leading up the bank to a stile C. Now the walk continues across the fields with the Wall to

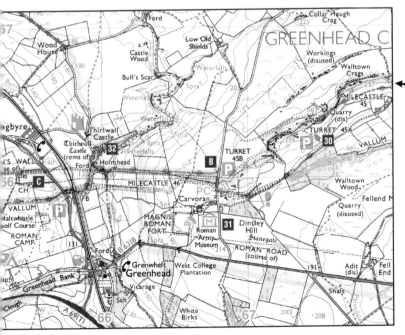

ntours are given in metres
he vertical interval is 10m

the right. Continue across the fields, passing a farm on your left. The route continues in a straight line to a stile in front of some prominent hummocks which leads on to a footbridge, and the line runs along the south side of the ditch. Beyond the next footbridge, the path leads around the farm buildings and then goes right across a garden; you tramp through watched by an army of gnomes. Continue along the farm track to the next stile, and then simply continue in a straight line across the fields. Head for the obvious gap in the row of houses at the edge of Gilsland. At the road **D** turn right and immediately left to continue along the path by the road. Once again there is a brief acquaintance with a cottage garden before the path returns to the fields and follows the minor road around to the left. Cross over the next road and continue on the footpath over the field opposite. After a little way turn towards the line of the railway on a path that dips down to the Poltross Burn, which is crossed by a single-arched viaduct carrying the line linking Newcastle and Carlisle.

The railway has a slightly odd history. The promoters were at first uncertain whether to build a railway or a canal, but when work was finally authorised in 1829, there was a proviso that on no account were any of those new-fangled steam locomotives to be used on the track. However, by the time it eventually opened throughout in 1851, steam was allowed. An unpromising start, but unlike many of Britain's lines, this one is at least still open.

Thirlwall Castle perched high on its grassy motte.

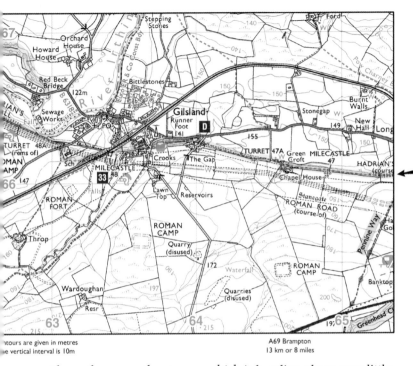

A69 Brampton
13 km or 8 miles

The path crosses the stream, which is bustling along over little falls, and rather to one's surprise the Wall puts in an appearance. Here, too, are the remains of Milecastle 48 **33**, which has yielded some useful information to archaeologists. Inside the walls are a few steps of what must have been a staircase up to the walkway. Extrapolating the line of the stairs to the point where they would meet the Wall suggests it was built to a height of around 15 feet.

From the milecastle take the narrow path between the field and the railway, and then cut across the line. Take the path down the railway embankment and join the stone-flagged path heading down by the houses to the road. Gilsland village is down to the right, and offers a variety of amenities. There was a time when it offered a lot more, for during a brief period of glory it was developed as a spa. Meanwhile, the line for the next section of walk is easily recognised. Cross over the road and take the path beside the length of exposed Wall and the well-preserved outline of Turret 48A. You can still see where part of the Wall has collapsed down the steep river bank, but other parts still rise to a height of over 3 feet (1 metre). This is a very pleasant section through farmland, with the River Irthing as a close companion.

Follow the path around the end of the barns and continue with the Wall on your left. There is a fine prospect, with a steep wooded bank rising on the far side of the river, mature trees dotted among the fields and a good section of Wall by the path. The Wall comes to an abrupt end with a lot of masonry on view **34**. In fact, the river has changed course and the masonry represents the abutments of the Roman bridge. This is a rather confused scene to interpret. It would appear that the river, which makes a great sweeping curve at this point, was steadily eroding the bank centuries ago, so that adjustments had to be made to the bridge. The Wall seems to have ended in the turret, its course to this point marked by the smaller stones. Then comes an extension built of far bigger stones, with two culverts. It has been suggested that these carried leats for a water mill, but very little physical evidence survives on the site to support this argument. At a later date a separate pier was added nearer to the present course of the river. It is all very intriguing, and matters are not helped by the absence of any surviving structural stones on the opposite bank.

The Roman bridge may have gone, but a new river crossing has been added in the shape of a modern footbridge, gently arcing across the water. The shape may have been dictated by the fact that the two banks of the river are not at the same level, but this really is a most elegant solution to the problem. Once across the bridge, go through the gate on the right to take the stone-flagged path running up the hill, which soon doubles back on itself. From the top of the rise, there is a lovely view of the broad sweep of the river valley and its lonely farmstead. The walk now continues from Milecastle 49 along the line of the Wall to Birdoswald. Those with extremely good eyesight may like to see if they can spot the various inscriptions carved in the Wall along this stretch. They can be found slightly more than halfway between the milecastle and the point where the minor road reaches the Wall; the best indicator is a large stone in the Wall of a brownish colour. There lies the centurial stone of Julius Primus and a well-defined phallus. The latter is not the Roman equivalent of graffiti, but a charm to keep the evil eye away. Leave via the kissing gate at the end of the tree-lined path to reach the roadside.

One of the great charms of this walk is that one might think before setting out that there is no need to stop and look at every fort along the way, because they must all be more or less the same, and up to a point they are. However, each comes with its own variation on the broader theme, and this is certainly true at Birdoswald **35**. Recent excavations have revealed a history for the site that shows a continuous story of occupation extending on for a long time after Roman rule came to an end. The starting point for a visit has to be the museum, which provides an introduction not just to the fort itself but also to the continuing work of archaeologists on the site. At this point the original Wall was built of turf, with turf milecastles. The site was no doubt chosen for its excellent defensive position, overlooking a steep drop down to the river. A stone turret was included in this structure. This was demolished to make way for the present fort. Among the features to note are the gateways. The west gate has well-dressed stones in the wall of the southern guard house. These are considerably bigger than those usually found along the Wall, and it seems likely that they were originally cut for use in a monument of some kind. The east gate has the most considerable masonry remains of any of the fort gateways on the Wall, with the door jamb on one side rising right

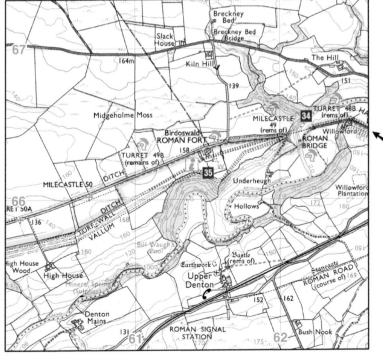

Contours are given in metres
The vertical interval is 10m

up to the springing of the arch. The north portal of the east gate was later blocked in. This presumably followed the rebuilding of the Wall in stone. The original fort had straddled the Turf Wall; the new Wall in stone passed along the northern edge. Inside the fort the paved granaries are very impressive, but not everything on view is Roman. In the Dark Ages a hall was built within the protection of the walls. Later dwellers on this troubled frontier looked for protection. A pele tower was raised near the west gate, of which quite considerable masonry remains can still be seen. In time this became a fortified farm, and then, as peace came to the area, the farm became just a comfortable home. Then, in the 19th century, the house was improved and a tower was added in imitation of the older tower. So building ended with a false fortification dominating the original defences built almost two millennia earlier.

The route follows the road in front of the fort and at the far side turns left through a kissing gate. At the wooded area it passes through a restored Victorian orchard and then doubles

The 19th-century tower is an imposing presence at Birdoswald fort.

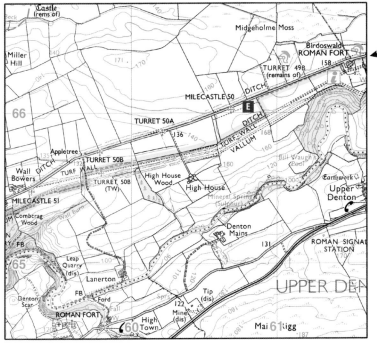

Contours are given in metres
The vertical interval is 10m

back beside the hedge to reach the road again. Now the walk continues in the field alongside the road. There is a neatly gravelled turret, showing that the road is following the line of the Stone Wall. Where signs of the Wall peter out, turn left along the stone wall, then right over a stone stile **E**, and continue the walk along the fence running beside the earthworks of the Turf Wall. This part of the walk is very straightforward as far as direction-finding is concerned, but it is not quite what it might seem. These ditches and humps seem quite like sections of Vallum met earlier along the way, but this is much more complex. Immediately next to the path is the ditch, but beyond that is the very distinct line of the Turf Wall, with the Vallum right alongside to the south. The later Stone Wall is still on the line of the road to the north. At the second farm track, turn left down to the footbridge over the Wall Burn, and continue the walk with the Vallum now on the right, heading for the trees. From here there are extensive views over to the south and the distant fells. Follow the line of the fence to reach a gate leading into the wood and continue in the same direction through the trees. At

101

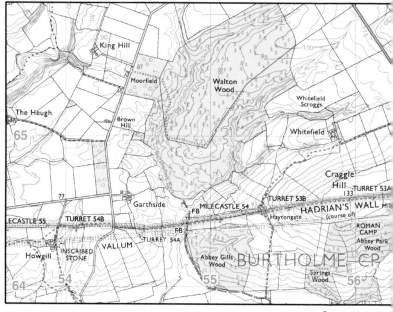

Contours are given in m
The vertical interval is

the far side, turn right alongside the wall to reach the road **F**. Turn left, and confirmation that the path is back with the Stone Wall comes in the shape of a turret. Immediately beyond the single-storey house there is a stile giving access to the fields again. Another turret appears, but the walk continues steadily forward, crossing a series of gated stiles in the walls.

On reaching the line of trees **G** look for the stile in the corner of the field and join the road to go around the farm. This is a very sturdy building and the older parts still have stone slate roofs. Once past the buildings, cross the next stile to resume walking along the field. Now take the gate in the corner of the field, not the more obvious farm gate, to arrive at the Pike Hill signal tower **36**. It is obviously carefully sited as it offers immense vistas over a wide tract of country. It was, equally obviously, in existence before the construction of the Wall. It is not aligned square with the Wall, as all the turrets have been, and as a result the Wall has a distinct kink in it to incorporate this useful structure.

Beyond the signal station cross a stile to continue the walk on the field path beside the road for a short way, but then rejoin the road for the walk through the village. Up ahead there is a real sense of the land beginning to flatten out, and there is a

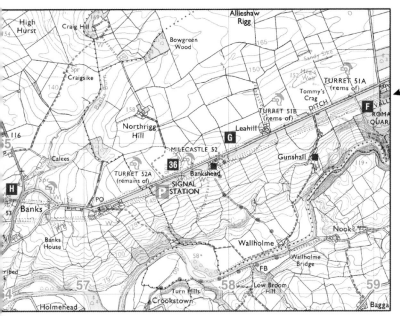

ours are given in metres
e vertical interval is 5m

good deal to look at closer at hand. An attractive single-storey cottage is dated 1834 – clearly it was once not a single house but a short terrace – and it is pleasing to see a converted farmhouse a little further on with well-carved stone mullions. Where the road divides, turn right, then left at the T-junction. Take the first turning on the right **H**, towards Hare Hill.

There is immediate confirmation that you are on the right route as a short section of Wall appears. The roadway dips down into a little valley and climbs back out again. Where the surfaced track swings right by a house with rendered walls, carry on through a kissing gate. Keep to the edge of the field and leave by the gate to continue on the farm track running between fence and hedge. You are now back amid arable land again, with the views to the south rather blocked by large patches of conifers. This is an altogether gentler farming landscape, though there are still the occasional patches of coarse moorland grasses. Between the patches of woodland the scenery is all very pleasant, the farmland well supplied with trees of all kinds from modest hawthorn to fine mature oak. Passing a very substantial farmhouse, cross over the drive and continue on the path between fence and hedgerow. Another

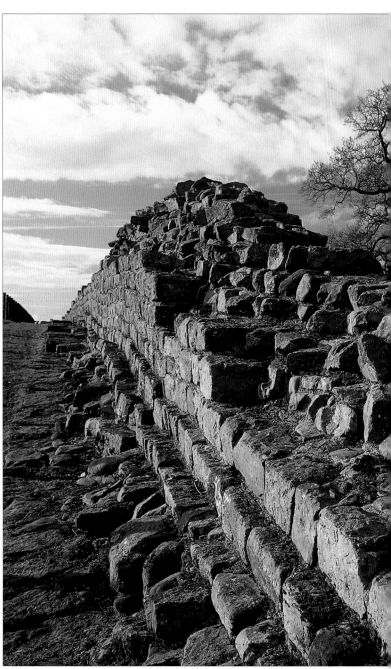
A well-preserved section of Wall on the walk between Gilsland and Birdoswald.

large patch of conifers looms up on the left and the path continues steadily downhill. For a time the only hint of the Wall is the slightly raised ground. The route leads down to a footbridge and then continues straight on up the field. Now, however, there are signs of stonework in the field bank to the right, and the occasional squared stone block can be seen tumbled into the field. Some of the stones even appear to carry traces of white mortar. What we are actually looking at is the very core of the Wall itself, exposed to view. The path climbs to an area of rough, reedy grassland where stone slabs have been laid to ease the walker's way across some of the wetter areas.

Cross straight over the road and turn right towards a kissing gate. Continue across the next field to another kissing gate to the right of the dead tree, and cross the farm approach road. Carry on through the fields. At the minor road keep walking across in the same direction past Hollybush Cottage to a kissing gate, then follow the hedge to turn right I down to the stream. Turn left along the bank to a kissing gate. Join the road and turn right to cross the bridge and follow the road up into Walton.

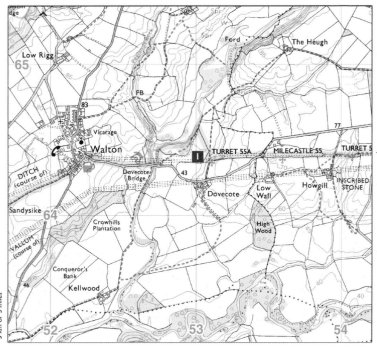

Contours are given in metres
The vertical interval is 5m

John Clayton

Most visitors who are not intending to walk the whole of Hadrian's Wall head first for the central section where the scenery is wild and the Wall itself well preserved. For this they owe a big thank-you to John Clayton. Born in 1792, he entered his father's law firm as a young man and by 1832 was at its head. He was also town clerk for Newcastle in the 1830s at a time of rapid development. But it was staying at the family's country house at Chesters that introduced him to the Wall and fired him with enthusiasm for its study and preservation. He saw at first hand how local farmers were helping themselves to the stones and he was determined to put a stop to this. He had no powers to prevent farmers doing as they wished on their own land, so he began a programme of buying up the farms. In 1834 he started purchasing property around Steel Rigg, and eventually he had gained control of land from Acomb Fell near Brunton in the east to Cawfields in the west. This included such important sites as Chesters, Carrawburgh, Housesteads and Vindolanda.

Clayton was concerned that Hadrian's Wall should be seen in all its grandeur, uncluttered by later developments. Farms that sat right on the Wall were demolished and replaced by new buildings a short distance away. Little now remains of the 17th-century farmhouse at Housesteads, but a new house was built in a neo-Tudor style a little to the south. It is somehow a very Victorian idea to knock down an old house and replace it with one designed to look even older, though it has to be said that the farmer got far better facilities with the change. Clayton built judiciously and managed his new estates with considerable skill, improving both the land and the livestock. His main objective may have been to preserve the Wall, but good management ensured that there was cash to spare for more active involvement in excavation and restoration.

Clayton began his excavations near his Chesters home, on the fort of Cilurnum, in 1843. The overall pattern of the site was soon revealed, and detailed work was started on the praetorium, the commander's house, and on the bath house. In the course of this work a stone was uncovered bearing the name of the Twentieth Legion, who were known to be in Britain during Hadrian's reign. It was positive evidence that the Wall was not, as had been generally believed, begun by Severus. Work continued on excavating milecastles and then proceeded to Housesteads. This

That we can enjoy sights such as this, at Housesteads, is due to the example set by John Clayton, who began rebuilding parts of the Wall in the 19th century.

attracted so much popular interest that most of the excavations were filled in again to prevent further damage by eager tourists.

The best-known part of Clayton's work, which we can still see today, is what archaeologists call the Clayton Wall. He set his workmen the task of reconstructing long sections of the Wall itself, generally to a height of seven courses. First, the debris was cleared away and facing stones were used to build up a dry-stone wall with a rubble infill. The top was covered by locally cut turf. Almost the only way in which the Clayton Wall can be distinguished from original Roman work is by the mortar still visible between the stones in the original. The best of Clayton's work can be seen along Housesteads Crags. Later restoration has produced what is known as the Consolidated Wall, using modern mortar. Some experts prefer the Clayton method, as it causes less damage to the core by allowing it to 'breathe'. It suffers, however, from the very real disadvantage that it collapses quite quickly if walked on.

John Clayton was a man of great vision, but at his death the estate passed to a nephew who preferred gambling to archaeology. Sadly, his horses seldom won and opponents generally held better cards. By 1929 most of the estate had been put up for sale to pay off his debts. There was no purchaser for Housesteads and in 1930 it was given to the National Trust. This was the start of a process that was to see the Trust acquiring ever more land, continuing a tradition begun by an enthusiastic Newcastle lawyer. There is one memorial that would surely have pleased him. At Wallington Hall, near Morpeth, there is a series of paintings by William Bell Scott, portraying aspects of Northumbrian life. One shows the building of the Wall under the direction of a centurion. He has been given the face of John Clayton.

5 Walton to Carlisle

via Crosby-on-Eden
11 miles (17.8 km)

Walton is a pleasant little village with a large green and a rather unprepossessing Victorian church with a square tower. Walk past, or pause at, the Centurion Inn and then, where the road bends **A**, turn right down the track that leads out into the fields. Carry on with the hedge to the left. On reaching the woodland, go through the kissing gate to the right of the farm. This takes you into the wood, over a stone-slab bridge, and then there is a very obvious path through the trees. The path's surface varies between bark and stone slabs, and, looking at the soggy surrounds and standing pools, one feels suitably grateful. This is a particularly attractive wood, especially in spring when the bluebells flourish. Reaching the edge of the wood, turn right onto the farm road, and at the minor road **B** turn immediately left up the farm track, where a welcoming committee of dogs can usually be found waiting. Keep straight on past the farm, and after a short way turn right through a kissing gate with the line of the Wall now reappearing to the left of the path. At the

The fertile landscape to the east of Walton.

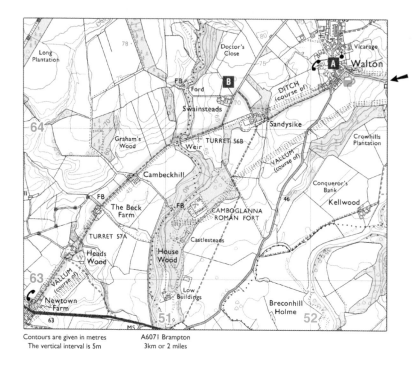

Contours are given in metres   A6071 Brampton
The vertical interval is 5m   3km or 2 miles

end of the field take the stone-flagged path down to the copse
and the footbridge over the Cam Beck. This is a most attractive
spot, with sandstone bluffs rising above the water and a noisy
weir just downstream of the bridge.

Once over the river, turn left to follow the fence towards the
farm buildings. Go through the yard between the barns and continue across the next field, with the hedge on the left, to reach a
gate in the far corner. This leads to a footbridge over the stream.
Turn right upstream to the next gate and turn left around the
farm buildings. Once clear of the buildings, turn right again to
follow the path beside the hedge to a flight of sandstone steps
leading up the hill. The path passes a handsome sandstone
house, which actually stands on the remains of an old motte and
bailey, then heads for a gate in the corner. Again the walk continues along the line of a hedge, but this time, by way of variation,
the hedge is on the right. This is mainly flat grazing land, the
fields dotted with sturdy oaks, but there is still a distant prospect
of hills out to the south. The route is now down a little lane
between the fields, which ends at the outskirts of Newtown,
where the last stage crosses the end of a garden.

111

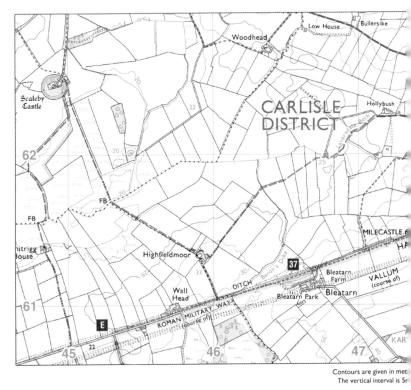

Contours are given in met
The vertical interval is 5r

The path emerges by a green. Cross straight over the road and continue on the road opposite. This is indeed a new town: a little bit of suburbia dropped into the countryside. At the road junction keep to the left, then as the road turns sharp left **C** carry straight on to take the path through the field, with the fence to the left. After the first field cross to the opposite side of the fence and continue in the same direction. At this point the Wall ditch again becomes a prominent landscape feature. Ignore the broad track heading off to the right and waymarked by an arrow; instead, continue through a kissing gate to join a narrow little lane **D**. Up ahead there is a first glimpse of the taller buildings of Carlisle, with a background of hills. At the hamlet of Old Wall there are two old buildings given very different treatments. The first is a farm and its surrounding barns, left as they were built, with the rich red of the sandstone giving a warmth to the otherwise plain buildings. Adjoining Old Wall Cottage has been painted white; the effect is crisply dramatic and no less attractive.

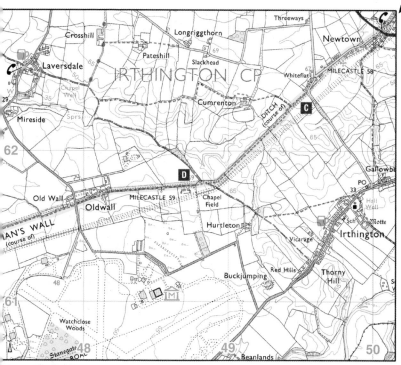

ontours are given in metres
The vertical interval is 5m

Cross over the road and continue in a dead-straight line across
the fields. It is not apparent, but the walk is still following the line
of Hadrian's Wall, with the Wall ditch to the right and the Vallum
a little further away to the south. On the approach to Bleatarn
Farm the walk crosses a farm track and, just for a change, goes
across the middle of the field. Here there is a complex pattern of
earthworks, with the long ridge in the middle of the field defining
the line of the Wall **37**. It is a moment to savour, for it is the last
trace of the Wall we shall be seeing for some time. Leave the field
for a lane that leads directly down to the road. At the farm continue straight on along the minor road, which runs straight as a
die, as one would expect, for this was built right over the course of
the Wall (which explains why there is nothing in the way of physical remains to be seen). Carry on past a solitary cottage on the left,
and then after a little way turn left down a broad track **E**. A little
farther on the surfaced track gives way to a grassy lane running
between hedgerows, which turns out to be a highway for rabbits
hopping cheerfully along until they spot the intruder. It is all very

113

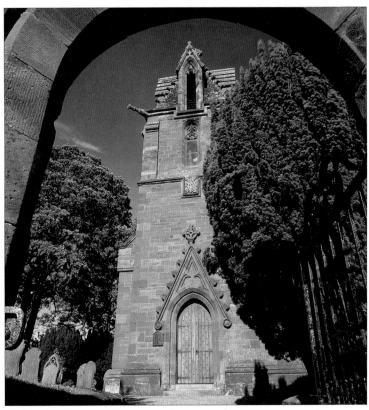
Crosby church, almost lost among the surrounding trees.

pleasant, and would be more so but for the ever-increasing sound of traffic on the busy A689. On reaching a plantation of saplings, follow the path around the edge to the right to reach the bridge across the main road. The bridge appears to be mainly used by cattle, which makes it somewhat aromatic, but it is at least a lot safer than trying to dash across the traffic down below.

Where the farm track swings away to the left, carry straight on to reach the road and turn right onto the pavement **F**. The walk goes past the very grand old vicarage, renamed Crosby Mansion, and the route is now running along the line of the Stanegate. The church stands at the edge of the village, a somewhat gloomy building surrounded by tall horse chestnuts rising as high as the spire. The 19th-century school next door looks rather like an estate lodge, with mouldings over the windows and a neat little belfry. Immediately past the Stag Inn turn left down the dead-end road and carry straight on down the track to arrive at the River Eden. Turn right to follow the path along the river bank. Now there is a very open aspect. The river itself is mainly placid, but occasionally breaks into little flurries of activity. There is a short diversion as the path turns away towards the prominent clump of trees and crosses a footbridge over the beck close by a solitary hawthorn. Carry on up to the trees, some of which are beautiful specimens, including some gorgeously bronzed copper beech. The trees may be attractive, but the sound emanating from them is rather less so, as they house a particularly raucous rookery. The house behind this imposing shelter **38** is all but overwhelmed by its immense portico, which is definitely not in proportion to the house. After that the path returns to the river bank.

One of the pleasures of any riverside walk is to be found in the bird life, which changes with the seasons, but in early summer there is a pleasant contrast between the idling swans and the frantically busy swallows dashing to and fro above the water. Where the way ahead is blocked by a fence **G** turn right onto the obvious track, go through the gate, and turn left where the way divides.

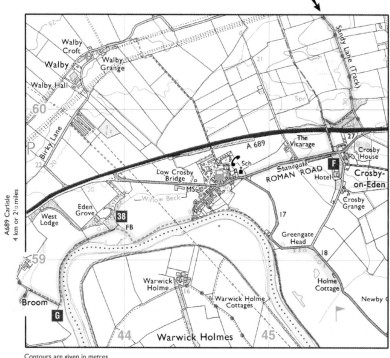

Contours are given in metres
The vertical interval is 5m

The main view up ahead is now of the traffic crossing the river on the motorway bridge. Continue in the same direction on the track signposted to Linstock. The river, which has been off on a long meander, puts in a brief appearance before turning sharply away again. Carry on down the fine avenue of trees, and a rather gaunt-looking house, Linstock Castle, appears on the right. This is not so much a castle as a pele tower, a building typical of the border country. Local families could retreat to it for safety with as much of their possessions as they could carry to escape the frequent violent raids. The track emerges at a housing estate. Keep on in the same direction down the road opposite, past the mainly new houses spreading out along one side of a small green. As the houses come to an end, turn right to join the minor road, then left to cross the motorway. In the distance are the fells to the north of Keswick at the outer edge of the Lake District National Park.

The languid waters of the River Eden provide a pleasant accompaniment for much of the latter part of the walk.

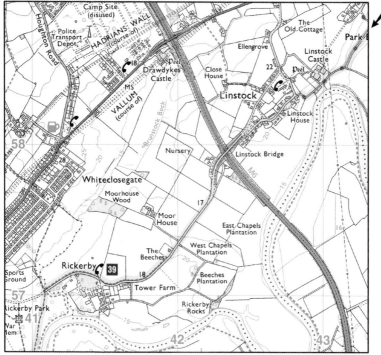

Contours are given in metres
The vertical interval is 5m

The walk continues down a little country lane, and as the traffic noise gradually diminishes, so the landscape becomes ever more attractive. There are a few houses along the way, including The Beeches, which earns its name by being surrounded by a beech hedge, while copper beech flourish in the grounds. Just beyond the house there is a welcome chance to leave the road for a cycle track and footpath running alongside it. Almost at once a rather curious set of buildings comes into view **39**. First comes an estate house with stepped gables, followed by Tower Farm, which obviously gets its name from the square turret that adorns it. Even odder is an isolated tower in the middle of the field on the right. The man with an obsession for turrets and towers was a gentleman with the unlikely name of George Head Head, who lived in Rickerby House when folly building was all the rage in the early 19th century. The porticoed gatehouse a little further along has a coat of arms put there by Head bearing the motto 'Study Quiet', which became particularly apt when a girls' school was opened here.

Crossing over a tributary of the Eden brings you to parkland and the end of the cycle track. From here turn left down the tarmac path, with the war memorial over to the right, to head for the footbridge across the Eden. It is a fairly plain steel bridge, but the engineers and city worthies who paid for it were sufficiently proud of the project to record their names and the date of opening, 1922, for posterity. On the other side turn right onto the riverside path. Where the surfaced path comes to an end, continue on the grassy path at the water's edge. This is a pleasant stroll around the edge of a golf course, but sadly, being so close to 'civilisation', it is spattered with litter. The great bend of the river brings you back to a point where the war memorial of Rickerby Park can be seen just across the water. The path becomes quite rural, hemmed in by all kinds of plants, with hogweed, ragwort and ransom predominating. The river, which has been placid for some time, bursts into activity in a series of small falls at the shallows just in front of the road bridge. The stone bridge itself is a very grand affair, carried on five arches, and although it was widened in the 20th century, the style is still very much in keeping with the date at which it was first built, 1815. Passing under the bridge, the path now joins a broad walk down an avenue of horse chestnut that carries on beside the river. Many walkers, however, will no doubt be pausing here at Carlisle before the start of the last leg of the journey.

Carlisle has a great deal to offer, but there is only space here for a brief note on three sites. The most obvious visit is to Tullie House in Castle Street, which was built in the 17th century on the site of the Roman Stanegate fort, and contains the remains of a 3rd-century shrine within the grounds. There are many finds from different parts of Hadrian's Wall and several reconstructions, including a Roman street. Nearby is the castle, the oldest visible part of which was begun under Henry I in the 1120s and completed shortly afterwards by David I of Scotland. This is a good example of the changing fortunes of Carlisle itself, claimed by both the English and the Scots. The squat tower of the keep will be a prominent feature in the next part of the walk. The cathedral also shows signs of the long conflict that saw the armies surging backwards and forwards across the disputed border. The nave, with its immense stone columns, seems quintessentially Norman, but in fact only two of the bays near the chancel are original, the rest having been demolished following Scottish attacks in the wars of 1645 and 1652. One masterpiece of carving, the Salkeld Screen, created in the 1540s, miraculously survived the onslaught, as did the remarkable Augustine screen in the south aisle. This consists of a series of 22 panels showing episodes in the life of the saint, including a picture of an understandably nervous-looking Augustine confronting a demon with a second horned head coming out of his backside. If nothing else, these visits confirm Carlisle's key role in the centuries of border conflicts that lasted long after the Romans' departure.

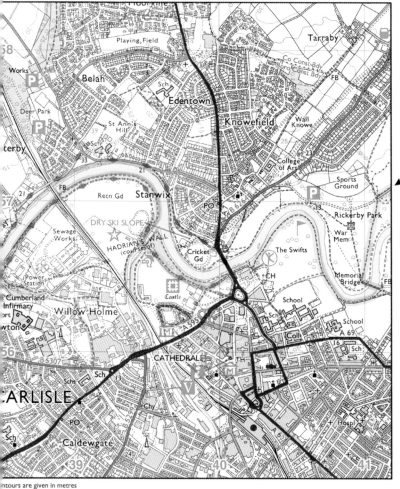

ntours are given in metres
he vertical interval is 5m

Reivers and Farmers

The end of Roman civilisation did not instantly usher in a new age of barbarism. The Dark Ages did not get their name because they were a time of infamous deeds, but simply because comparatively little is known about life at that time. That is certainly true of the area surrounding Hadrian's Wall. No written evidence survives, and most of what we can surmise about the period immediately following the Roman withdrawal comes from the specialist researches of palaeobotanists. If there had been a general collapse of settlements as the troops withdrew, then cereal crops would no longer have been sown and the forest would gradually have crept back over the abandoned lands. This happened to some extent, but only slowly, and there is a good deal of evidence that Vindolanda and Birdoswald, at least, continued to be occupied. When it comes to the Anglo-Saxon period, evidence becomes almost non-existent.

The medieval period saw the area around Hadrian's Wall reverting to what it had been in Roman times: a frontier zone, but one no longer subject to strict controls imposed by a powerful army. People had to look to their own defences. Out of this dangerous time, amid constant skirmishes between the Scots and the English, came the pele (or peel) towers. These massive stone buildings, three or four storeys high, had a single, heavily guarded entrance to a ground-floor storage area, with the upper storeys and living quarters approached by a narrow stairway. These were not castles designed to keep an army at bay, but they did offer stout protection from the armed bands of border raiders, or reivers. The remains of such a tower can be seen at Steel Rigg. A close relation to the pele tower was the bastle house, which was a fortified farmhouse and notably less grim in appearance. One of the finest examples is Drumburgh Castle. It was built in 1307, inevitably using stones from the Wall, and it was enlarged during the reign of Henry VIII, when it became the headquarters of the Barony of Burgh. In houses such as this, animals were kept on the ground floor, and the living quarters of the house were reached via a retractable ladder, later replaced by an external staircase. Drumburgh's former importance is indicated by heraldic carving over the main entrance, and a Roman altar in the front garden shows its borrowings from antiquity.

Pele towers and bastle houses are strong evidence of the wildness of the times, and the Wall itself was again brought into use when watchmen were appointed at lookout posts to warn of cross-border marauders. It was not a simple case of the Scots mounting raids on the English and vice versa: there was no shortage of border families prepared to make a good living from banditry, cattle raids and horse stealing. Few areas had a more fearsome reputation than the country around Housesteads. The remains of a bastle house and a farmhouse can be identified near the old fort, and it was here that the notorious Armstrong clan settled after being driven out of Scotland in the 17th century. Their reign of infamy ended when Nicholas Armstrong was hanged in 1704 and his brothers escaped to America.

Although violence was a fact of life along the border, it was not the whole of life. Crops were still grown, and the ridge and furrow of old field systems can still be seen. One feature, in particular, that began in the early medieval period was to last for many centuries: transhumance, based on shielings. In this system, cattle and sheep were brought up from the fertile valleys in the spring to graze on the rough moorland, and there they stayed until autumn. The meadows, freed from the attention of munching livestock, were able to yield a rich grass crop, which was then harvested for winter feed to be used when the beasts returned. The herdsmen and their families stayed with their charges right through the summer, living out in the shielings. These were generally long, low, windowless huts, built with dry-stone walls and topped with turf roofs. There are remains of many shielings along the Wall, with one of the largest groups of 15 buildings being found near Greenlea Lough. The word itself survives in place names such as Highshield and Sewing Shields.

Violence and lawlessness inhibited development; real change only began with the Act of Union, which brought official, if not actual, peace to the borders. It was the building of the Military Road that finally made it possible to enforce that peace. But even in the late 18th century the area was still one of small farmsteads and large commons. The Enclosure Acts brought neatness and order to much of the countryside, but this policy was only slowly introduced in the North. Modernisation of farming methods made a real impact in the 19th century, thanks to the enthusiasm of men like John Clayton. It was then that the present pattern of fields began to emerge, but it is still possible to trace the long history of farming all the way back to the first marks of the plough, the cord rig, the shallow scratches on the ground of prehistoric farmers.

6 Carlisle to Bowness-on-Solway

via Burgh by Sands, Drumburgh and Glasson
14 3/4 miles (23.8 km)

At the far side of the bridge there is a formal park, and the official route follows the broad pathway. There is an alternative, informal path: go down the steps to join the riverside trail. This is a pleasant, tree-lined walk and new trees have been planted so that in time there will be an even greater sense of seclusion, away from the city noises. There is one brief glimpse of the castle, looking suitably forbidding, and then the city is largely left behind. Along the way, the walk passes a rock garden, not in the traditional sense but a garden consisting entirely of rocks and stones. The path turns up the side of the River Caldew and the two routes unite at the bridge that leads to a sports ground and athletics track. Continue around the edge of the field to rejoin the riverside walk. The high bank on the far side of the river is covered in trees and a wide variety of plants and shrubs line the path. A second bridge appears up ahead, carrying the West Coast Main Line rail route up to Scotland. This is a very utilitarian structure, with iron girders on unadorned stone piers. With increased traffic, the old bridge proved inadequate, and an even more utilitarian concrete bridge was built alongside it. Having assumed that the city had

Carlisle Castle, begun by Henry I and 'modernised' by Henry VIII.

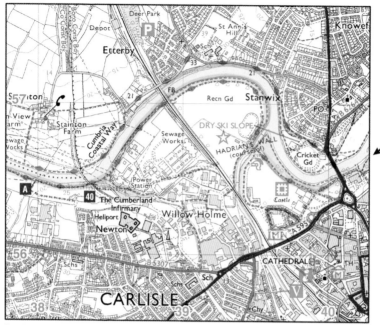

Contours are given in metres
The vertical interval is 5m

been left behind, it is a little disconcerting to discover that this was merely due to the river having left the city on a wide bend; the path has now come right back to the far-from-appealing outskirts. Here are an old power station, a sewage works and a dump, a combination which gives a general air of dereliction and exudes some very unpleasant aromas. If it does nothing else, this short section quickens your pace as you hurry to get past.

Happily, this is only a brief interlude, and the walk now passes the remains of an old bone mill before arriving at a second railway bridge **40**. This is a much more elegant affair than the last and was built to carry the tracks of the Border Union Railway, opened in 1859 but now closed. Look up at the arch as you walk underneath and you can see that it was built on the skew, with bricks laid in diagonal courses. At the far side of the bridge climb the steps made out of old sleepers. The walk now continues as a tree-shaded lane on the top of the bank. This section, with its silver birch and brightly flowering broom, is doubly welcome after the short urban encounter. A set of stone-flag steps **A** leads down to a bridge across a stream, followed by a climb back up through the trees to rejoin the walk on top of the river bank.

The path stays close to the calm waters of the River Eden on the approach to Grinsdale.

The path leads along the edge of the field, with the river just visible as occasional flashes of light through the trees that line the high bank. There is a brief renewal of acquaintance as steps lead down to the water's edge and immediately climb back up the other side of the dip. Follow the line of the hawthorn hedge to a gate in the corner of the field. This leads to a narrow path through the wood that winds down to a footbridge and then climbs again to run above the steep bank. After that it is a return to walking across fields, bright with meadow flowers of many different species. The walk now turns away from the river to skirt around a clump of trees and then heads towards the village of Grinsdale. Take the footbridge across the stream, which at some times of the year has the appearance of an elongated pond, and continue up to the road **B**, passing a group of new houses. Turn right along the road, and after a short way turn left at the kissing gate by the barn. Cross the stile by the gate between the barns and take the obvious farm track, and keep following it as it swings round to the left. Keep ahead with the hedge on your left and cross a small footbridge. At this point a faint dip can be seen crossing the field on the left **41**. This is the Vallum, a useful reminder that the path is still following the line of Hadrian's Wall.

Crossing the next stile brings you to the top of a bank, looking down at a field marked with the signs of ridge and furrow. Continue along the top of the bank, with a view out over a patchwork of fields on the river plain. Just before reaching the farm gate, turn left over two stiles to keep to the top of the little bank and follow the path beside the field and the extensive stables before making your way down to a stile beside the duckpond. Once over the stile, turn left and then immediately right **C**. The walk continues beside the stream, and after a long absence the river returns. Now the path climbs to the top of a wooded

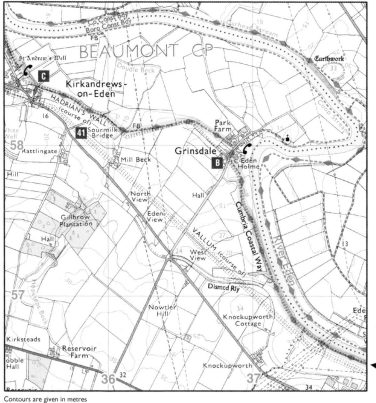

Contours are given in metres
The vertical interval is 5m

bank above the river and then descends again on an undulating course, twisted by landslips over the years. The path stays with the river until it reaches the road, where you turn left towards the centre of Beaumont. If the riverside path is still closed, there will be a clearly marked diversion along the road. Coming up into the village from the river, the church **42** appears standing on a mound, the *beau mont* itself. It is well worth pausing here. The Wall came right through this site and the Normans used the stones to build the church, though it has been greatly altered since then. The more obvious Norman sections are the south doorway and the arcading at the east end. A Roman inscription can be seen across the road in the wall opposite Hilltop Cottage.

The walk continues down the road signposted to Burgh by Sands, then after a short way, just before the black-and-white house, turns left onto the footpath. This leads into a straight, broad path set directly on the course of the Wall. It is not immediately obvious, but there is now a long steady climb. The hilltop may be only a modest 30 metres above sea level, but in this very flat landscape it makes it almost a mountain, and it certainly opens up the view out to the hills of Scotland. The rutted farm track eventually gives way to a grassy lane and then finally opens out into the fields. The route carries straight on in the same direction, between the line of trees on the right, to

The church at Burgh by Sands incorporates a 14th-century fortified tower.

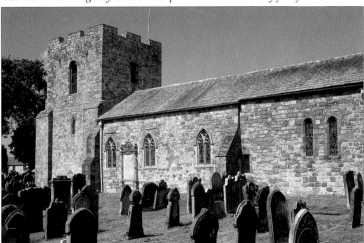

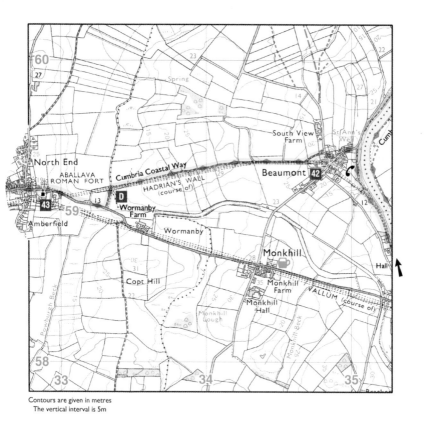

Contours are given in metres
The vertical interval is 5m

reach a footbridge **D**. Once over the bridge, turn left on the path down to the road and turn right towards Burgh by Sands.

The village stands on the site of the Roman fort of Aballava, which means apple orchard. There is very little trace of either fort or Wall, and the earthworks are those of the far more recent railway and canal. Reaching the centre of the village, the walk passes St Michael's Church, another building of great historical significance **43**. As it lies within the boundary of the old fort, there was no shortage of good building stone; even when the original church was completed in the 12th century, there was still enough left in the area for Roman stones to be incorporated into the later tower. The builders of the 12th century were not very particular about which stones they used nor how they used them. As a result, this Christian church contains the carved head of a pagan god inside the chancel on the east wall. The greatest change to the church came in the 14th century, following the death of Edward I. He had attempted to subjugate the Scots and had enjoyed some success in the Lowlands, but his successors were unable to hold on to what he had won. The result was a long period of border warfare and raids, during which ordinary people had to look to their own resources for protection. Wealthy families built pele towers, but some churches also provided peles for the population. The fortified tower was built in the 14th century, and the only entrance is from inside the church through a small door protected by an iron gate. The road turning off to the right beyond the church leads to the Edward I monument, out on the marshes where the king died, not in battle but from dysentry while waiting to cross the Solway Firth.

The walk carries straight on down the main street, and there is a lot of interest along the way. Building materials in the older houses vary from sandstone, which has been such a feature of the eastern end of the walk, to brick, sometimes arranged in a chequered effect known as diaper work. The houses begin to thin out and the road is now following a line to the south of the Vallum, though there is very little even to hint at its presence, still less that of the Wall beyond it. At the road junction **E** carry straight on to the cattle grid. Now here is a really unexpected sign. There seem to be fields on every side, but the sign announces the presence of a coastguard station. The next sign provides the explanation, declaring that the road is liable to flooding. In fact, it runs right out over the salt marshes, and at exceptionally high spring tides the whole area could be under many feet of water, as the depth posts beside the road indicate. So those who come this way on foot must be aware that this part of the walk could be impassable at certain times of the year when rivers swollen by rain combine with high tides. If in any doubt, check the tide tables for Port Carlisle, which are available from the tourist information office at Silloth (tel: 01697 331944), and the weather forecast – a south or southwesterly wind increases the chances of flooding. Tides come in very quickly, so try to set off either 3 hours before or $1^1/_2$ hours after high tide. There is no reason why this section should present a problem in normal circumstances provided walkers are aware of the dangers.

The walk now follows the line of the long, high embankment to the left of the road, following the path at the bottom of the slope. This has nothing to do with the Wall, but is in fact a sea-defence barrier, behind which is the line of the former railway from Carlisle to Port Carlisle. Originally the two places had been joined by canal, but in 1852 the decision was taken to

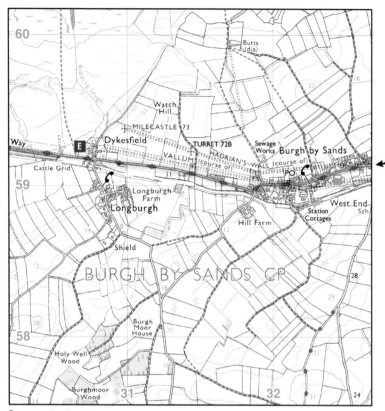

Contours are given in metres
The vertical interval is 5m

fill that in and build a railway over the top. There is no diffi-
culty here with route-finding as the line simply goes straight
ahead to distant Drumburgh. That does not mean, however,
that the section is without interest: far from it. To the south
there are views of the distant fells all the way across to the
shapely cone of Skiddaw; to the north are the huge expanses of
salt marshes and the sandbanks, where the flows of the Eden
and the Esk combine. Cattle graze the marshland, but the area
is chiefly notable for its population of seabirds and waders.
What one sees on the walk will very much depend on the state
of the tide, but among the many species one is almost certain
to see the bird that has been adopted as the symbol of the
Solway coast: the oystercatcher. It is easy to see why this is
such a local favourite, its spruce black-and-white plumage
contrasting with its orange beak and rather fetching pink legs.

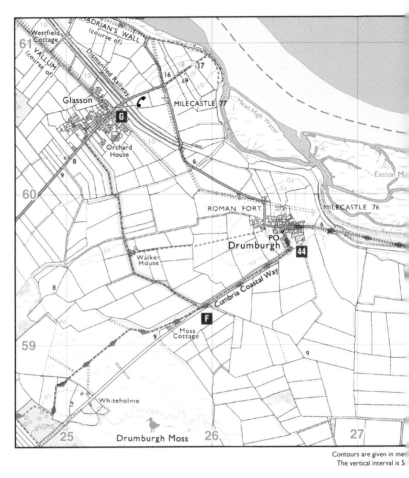

Contours are given in metres
The vertical interval is 5

There is a road junction connecting to Boustead Hill – not much of a hill, perhaps, but high enough to keep the villagers' toes out of the water.

This section of the walk ends at Drumburgh, which was the site of a small fort. The road passes Drumburgh Castle **44**, a fortified house, with an entrance at first-floor level only to make it easier to defend. It is sturdy and imposing, and its importance is confirmed by the heraldic birds carved over the entrance. It also has altar stones from a Roman temple as garden ornaments. Just beyond the castle turn left down the lane and follow it round to the right. Where the track divides before the cattle grid **F**, turn right onto another broad farm track, surrounded by a neat pattern of square fields. The track passes the

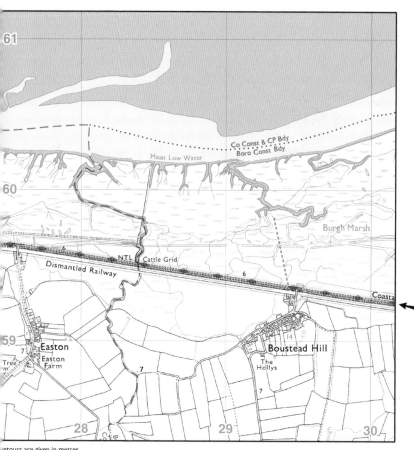

ntours are given in metres
he vertical interval is 5m

farm and a jumble of old machinery and then continues as a
path through the fields. Continue in the same direction as
before, with the fence and ditch to your right. There is one
slight, but obvious, kink, which takes the path to the footbridge
over the stream. After that there is a curious arrangement of
long, narrow fields strongly reminiscent of medieval strips. At
the road, turn right into Glasson, passing a converted chapel.
At the Highland Laddie pub **G**, so called because it is claimed
Bonnie Prince Charlie stopped here, turn left onto the green
way. This lies right along the line of the Vallum, and has been
recently improved, which, considering it acts as a drain for the
surrounding fields, is good news for walkers. At the caravan
park the track swings right to join the coast road.

The Rivers Eden and Esk combine to create the wide waters of the Solway Firth, an area with its own unique lonely beauty.

Cross over the road and join the path along the disused railway embankment to reach Port Carlisle. This was established in 1819 as a means of avoiding the difficult waters of the Solway Firth and was linked to Carlisle by canal. The remains of the entrance lock **45** can still be seen, as can the crumbling ruins of the breakwater. It had a short life, for the shifting sands made the port all but unusable; with the coming of the railway, a new steamer port was established further west at Silloth. Inland from the lock one can still see where the canal was replaced by the railway and Port Carlisle station. The path now rejoins the road for the final stretch right down on the shoreline up to Bowness-on-Solway, where Hadrian's Wall came to an end, running right down into the sea **46**. The actual end of the walk is reached by turning right off the main street to the sea wall, still referred to as The Banks. It could seem like an anticlimax, for the Wall itself has long since been eroded away here by the waves, but in fact this is a spot full of atmosphere, with the broad waters stretching away into the distance and Scotland in view on the far bank. It is still possible to recognise that this was once a wild frontier, and not just any frontier, but the most northerly of the whole Roman Empire. Although this was the end of the Wall, it was not the end of the Roman defensive system, for the line of milecastles and turrets, now known as milefortlets and towers, extended right along the shore of the Solway Firth as far as a fort at modern Maryport. It is also not quite the end of the story, for walkers will now be making their way into Bowness. It is still possible to see how the village was originally developed within the confines of the old fort, and there is a map on the wall of the King's Arms to help put everything in perspective. The overriding memory of this walk is of the contrasts, and they are nowhere more apparent than here at Bowness-on-Solway. The journey started on the edge of a great city under the shadow of shipyard cranes, and it has ended on this lonely shore with the cries of gulls and the gentle lap of the tide.

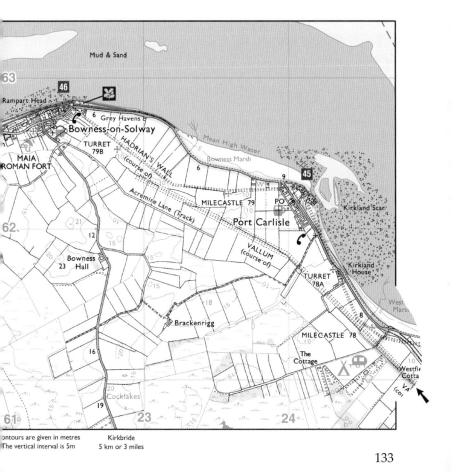

Contours are given in metres
The vertical interval is 5m

Kirkbride
5 km or 3 miles

The Solway Firth

The Firth is a wide estuary fed by the Esk from the north and the Eden from the south. The two rivers gouge channels through a vast expanse of sandy mudflats that lie gleaming and exposed at low water. The margins are characterised by salt marshes, and further inland are raised mires. These are extensive peat bogs, largely based on sphagnum moss that overlies the wetland as a soft, plump cushion of land. Each of these different areas has its own characteristics and supports its own plant population and wildlife.

The Firth itself is very shallow, but it is home to a rich and diverse fish population, many of which spawn in the area. Walkers will have few opportunities to see anything in the murky waters, though on a fine, calm day there is the chance of spotting an impressive, but harmless, basking shark. The waters are well known for their shellfish but most famous for salmon. Equally famous, in its own way, is the unusual method used for catching them: the Haaf net, introduced by the Vikings over a thousand years ago. The net itself is mounted on a wooden frame, generally 18 feet (6 metres) long and 5 feet (1.5 metres) high. The fisherman wades out into the water, holding the frame in front of him with the net itself streaming out behind as two pouches, one on each side of his body. When a fish hits the net, he has to whip the legs of the frame out of the water to trap the salmon, which is killed and stowed away in a bag. Haaf netters catch salmon and sea trout in a season that lasts from the end of February to early September. They can be seen working close to the shore anywhere between Sandsfield and Bowness-on-Solway.

The salt marshes and mudflats are a birdwatcher's delight. Ducks and geese abound and can be seen at their most numerous in winter, when huge flocks of pink-footed and barnacle geese fly down from the Arctic. In summer, the passing walker will certainly have a chance to see a rich variety of waders, including that most attractive of birds, the oystercatcher, with its black-and-white plumage setting off its brilliant-orange beak and pink legs. The marshes themselves provide a very mixed habitat, with their meandering creeks filling and emptying with the tide. The turf is particularly rich and soft and is still cut, particularly on Burgh Marsh, for surfacing bowling greens. It also provides rich grazing for cattle in summer and sheep in winter. The wide green expanses are enlivened by bursts of colour, from the rounded pink blooms of thrift to the brilliant scarlet of seablite, the latter an unusual plant that can quite happily survive being covered in sea water at high tide.

The region seems untroubled by time, but the modern world did put in an appearance in the 19th century. In 1819 an Act was passed for the construction of the Carlisle Canal. The aim was to bring cargo into Carlisle without the need for ships to negotiate the shifting channels of the Firth. The canal joined the sea at newly created Port Carlisle through three locks, which were needed to allow for the great tidal variations. According to the records available at the time, the highest water level had been reached in January 1796: over 15 feet (5 metres) above low tide.

The life of the canal was destined to be short. It was closed in 1853, and a railway was built over the old canal bed. That was not notably more successful, itself closing in 1932. Remains of both locks and old railway platforms can still be seen at Port Carlisle. A far more spectacular railway event occurred in 1869, when a viaduct was built across the Firth just to the west of Bowness, crossing the water to Annan. That closed even earlier, in the 1920s, but while it survived, the multi-arched viaduct effectively closed off the upper Firth for even the most modest coastal vessels. The railways closed, shipping never returned and the area was left comparatively remote and isolated. But what may have been bad news for some was certainly good news in terms of preserving a unique area of quiet, almost eerie beauty. Today's visitors may no longer hear the blast of the steam whistle, but in compensation they can enjoy the call of the curlew – not a bad exchange.

PART THREE

USEFUL INFORMATION

A booklet, *The Essential Guide to Hadrian's Wall Path National Trail*, gives information on facilities of all kinds, from cash points to toilets and from bus routes to secure car parking. It is available from Tourist Information Centres, price £1. It is regularly updated.

Transport

Information on transport to and from the Wall can be obtained from Tourist Information Centres. Also contact Traveline for all rail, coach and bus enquiries. Telephone 0870 608 2608. Minicom/textphone 0870 241 2216.

Rail
National Rail Enquiries, tel: 08457 484950.
Web: www.nationalrail.co.uk
Northern Rail, tel: 0845 00 00 125. Textphone: 0845 604 5608.
Web: www.northernrail.org
GNER, tel: 08457 225225. Minicom/textphone: 0191 221 3016.
Web: www.gner.co.uk
Virgin Trains, tel: 08457 222333. Minicom/textphone: 08457 443367.
Web: www.virgin.com/trains

Coach
National Express, tel: 08705 808080. Minicom/textphone: 0121 455 0086. Web: www.gobycoach.com

Local public transport
For public transport and Hadrian's Wall Bus enquiries, contact the Hadrian's Wall Information Line (telephone 01434 322002) or TICs.

Accommodation

A leaflet, *Where To Stay For Walkers*, is published by the National Trail Project and is available from Tourist Information Centres. This includes information on hotels, B&Bs, guesthouses, camping facilities and bunkhouses.

Youth Hostels
There are five youth hostels on or near the route. Further information can be obtained from the Youth Hostels Association, Trevelyan House, Dimple Road, Matlock, Derbyshire DE4 3YH. Tel: 0870 870 8868. E-mail: reservations@yha.org.uk. Web: www.yha.org.uk

Carlisle: Old Brewery Residences, Bridge Lane, Caldewgate, Carlisle, Cumbria CA2 5SR (open July–September). Tel: 0870 770 5752. E-mail: deec@impacthousing.org.uk GR 85/395560

Birdoswald: Birdoswald Roman Fort, Gilsland, Carlisle, Cumbria CA6 7DD. Tel: 0870 770 6124. E-mail: birdoswald@yha.org.uk

Greenhead: Station Road, Greenhead, Brampton, Cumbria CA8 7HG. Tel: 0870 770 5842. E-mail: greenhead@yha.org.uk GR 86/659655

Newcastle upon Tyne: 107 Jesmond Road, Newcastle upon Tyne NE2 1NJ. Tel: 0870 770 5972. E-mail: newcastle@yha.org.uk GR 88/257656

Once Brewed: Military Road, Bardon Mill, Northumberland NE47 7AN. Tel: 0870 770 5980. E-mail: oncebrewed@yha.org.uk GR 86/752668

Tourist Information Centres

Brampton*: The Moot Hall, Market Place, Brampton, Cumbria CA8 1RW. Tel: 01697 73433.

Carlisle: Old Town Hall, Green Market, Carlisle, Cumbria CA3 8JH. Tel: 01228 625600.

Corbridge*: Hill Street, Corbridge, Northumberland NE45 5AA. Tel: 01434 632815.

Haltwhistle/Hadrian's Wall Information Line: Railway Station, Station Road, Haltwhistle, Northumberland NE49 9HN. Tel: 01434 322002.

Hexham: Wentworth Car Park, Hexham, Northumberland NE46 1XD. Tel: 01434 652220.

Newcastle Tourist Information: 8–9 Central Arcade, Newcastle upon Tyne NE1 5BQ. Tel 0191 277 8000. Guildhall Visitor Information Centre, Newcastle Quayside, Newcastle upon Tyne NE1 3AF. Tel: 0191 277 8000.

Once Brewed*: Northumberland National Park Visitor Centre, Military Road, Bardon Mill, Hexham, Northumberland NE47 7AN. Tel: 01434 344396.

Prudhoe: Waterworld, Front Street, Prudhoe, Northumberland NE42 5DQ. Tel: 01661 833144.

Silloth-on-Solway: Solway Coast Discovery Centre, Liddell Street, Silloth-on-Solway, Cumbria CA7 4DD. Tel: 01697 33055.

* Open April to October only.

Useful Addresses

Countryside Agency, *see* Natural England

Cumbria Wildlife Trust, Brockhole, Windermere, Cumbria
LA23 1LJ. Tel: 01539 448280. E-mail: cumbriawt@cix.co.uk
Web: www.cumbriawildlifetrust.org.uk

English Heritage (North East), Bessie Surtees House,
41–44 Sandhill, Newcastle upon Tyne NE13 3JF.
Tel: 0845 301 0001/0191 261 1585.
E-mail: customers@english-heritage.org.uk
Web: www.english-heritage.org.uk

English Heritage (North West), Suite 3.3 & 3.4, Canada House,
3 Chepstow Street, Manchester M1 5FW. Tel: 0845 301 0002.
E-mail: customers@english-heritage.org.uk
Web: www.english-heritage.org.uk

Hadrian's Wall Heritage Ltd/National Trail Office, East Peterel
Field, Dipton Mill Road, Hexham, Northumberland, NE46 2JT.
Tel: 01434 609700. www.hadrians-wall.org.uk

Hadrian's Wall Information Line: 01434 322002.
Web: www.hadrians-wall.org.uk

National Trust (North East), Scots Gap, Morpeth,
Northumberland NE61 4EG. Tel: 01670 774691.
Web: www.nationaltrust.org.uk

National Trust (North West), The Hollens, Grasmere,
Ambleside, Cumbria LA22 9QZ. Tel: 01539 435599.
Web: www.nationaltrust.org.uk

*Natural England (Headquarters), John Dower House,
Crescent Place, Cheltenham GL50 3RA. Tel: 01242 521381
(for literature on all National Trails).

*Natural England, North East Regional Office, The Quadrant,
Newbrun Riverside, Newcastle upon Tyne NE15 8NZ.
Tel: 0191 229 5500. (for literature on National Trails and
other walks in the region).

Northumberland National Park Authority, Eastburn, South Park,
Hexham, Northumberland NE46 1BS. Tel: 01434 605555.
E-mail: admin@nnpa.org.uk. Web: nnpa.org.uk

Northumberland Wildlife Trust, The Garden House, St Nicholas
Park, Jubilee Road, Newcastle upon Tyne NE3 3XT.
Tel: 0191 284 6884. E-mail: northwildlife@cix.co.uk
Web: www.wildlifetrust.org.uk/northumberland

Ordnance Survey, Romsey Road, Maybush, Southampton
SO16 4GU. Tel: 08456 050505. Web: www.ordsvy.gov.uk

Ramblers' Association, Second Floor, Camelford House,
    87–90 Albert Embankment, London SE1 7TW.
    Tel: 020 7339 8511. Web: www.ramblers.org.uk
Royal Society for the Protection of Birds, The Lodge, Sandy,
    Bedfordshire SG19 2DL. Tel: 01767 680551.
    Web: www.rspb.org.uk
Weathercall (Meteorological Office)
    North East England: 09068 5004 18
    Cumbria & Lake District: 09068 5004 19
    Web: www.weathercall.co.uk
Youth Hostels Association, Trevelyan House, Dimple Road,
    Matlock, Derbyshire DE4 3YH. Tel: 0870 870 8868.
    Web: www.yha.org.uk

* Following the merger of the Countryside Agency and English Nature to form
Natural England in October 2006 these addresses may change. For updated
information visit www.naturalengland.org.uk

Bibliography

Alcock, Joan, *Life in Roman Britain*, English Heritage/Batsford,
    1996.
Bédoyère, Guy de la, *Hadrian's Wall: History and Guide*, Tempus,
    1998.
Bidwell, P.T., *Roman Forts in Britain*, English Heritage/Batsford,
    1997.
Bidwell, Paul, *Hadrian's Wall 1989–99*, South Shields, 1999.
Breeze, David J. and Dobson, Brian, *Hadrian's Wall*, 4th edn,
    Penguin, 2000.
Connolly, Peter, *The Legionary*, Oxford University Press, 1988.
—, *The Cavalryman*, Oxford University Press, 1988.
—, *The Roman Fort*, Oxford University Press, 1999.
Crow, James, *Book of Housesteads*, English Heritage/Batsford,
    1995.
— and Woodside, Robert, *Hadrian's Wall, An Historic Landscape*,
    The National Trust, 1999.
Davies, Hunter, *A Walk Along The Wall*, Weidenfeld & Nicolson,
    1984.
Embleton, Ronald and Graham, Frank, *Hadrian's Wall in the
    Days of the Romans*, Frank Graham, 1984.
Hutton, William, *The History of the Roman Wall*, 1813; reprinted
    as *The First Man to Walk Hadrian's Wall 1802*, Frank Graham,
    1990.

Places to Visit near the Wall

There are numerous Roman sites along the Wall, all of which will be featured in the walk description, and two important sites, Corbridge and Vindolanda, which are recommended as separate visits. The following list is of other sites of interest in the neighbourhood, listed in geographical order, from east to west.

South Shields
Arbeia Roman Fort and Museum
Jarrow
St Paul's Monastery (English Heritage) and Bede's World Museum
Newcastle upon Tyne
Museum of Antiquities
Bessie Surtees House (EH)
Newcastle Keep
Prudhoe Castle (EH)
Wylam
George Stephenson's Birthplace (National Trust)
Corbridge
Aydon Castle (EH)
Bardon Mill
Allen Banks Garden and Staward Gorge (NT)
Brampton
Lanercost Priory (EH)
Carlisle
Castle (EH)
Guildhall Museum
Tullie House Museum and Art Gallery

Ordnance Survey Maps covering Hadrian's Wall Path

Landranger (1:50 000): 85, 86, 87, 88
Explorer Outdoor Leisure (1:25 000): 43
Explorer (1:25 000): 314, 315, 316